The Buchanites : from first to last - Primary Source Edition

Train, Joseph, 1779-1852

Nabu Public Domain Reprints:

You are holding a reproduction of an original work published before 1923 that is in the public domain in the United States of America, and possibly other countries. You may freely copy and distribute this work as no entity (individual or corporate) has a copyright on the body of the work. This book may contain prior copyright references, and library stamps (as most of these works were scanned from library copies). These have been scanned and retained as part of the historical artifact.

This book may have occasional imperfections such as missing or blurred pages, poor pictures, errant marks, etc. that were either part of the original artifact, or were introduced by the scanning process. We believe this work is culturally important, and despite the imperfections, have elected to bring it back into print as part of our continuing commitment to the preservation of printed works worldwide. We appreciate your understanding of the imperfections in the preservation process, and hope you enjoy this valuable book.

T.2
10/5

# THE BUCHANITES

EDINBURGH: BALLANTYNE AND HUGHES,
PAUL'S WORK AND 3 THISTLE STREET.

ANDREW INNES.

"the timber soles of his clogs was to tak fire, his feet and legs micht be roasted, before he could shift the chair, or ony body come to his assistance"

THE BUCHANITES

FROM FIRST TO LAST.

BY

JOSEPH TRAIN,

AUTHOR OF "THE HISTORY OF THE ISLE OF MAN,"
&c. &c. &c.

"Here truth is told as strange as any fiction elsewhere found."—ANON.

"I never heard of alewife that turned preacher except Luckie Buchan in the West."—WAVERLEY NOVELS, vol. viii. p. 337, Abb. Ed.

WILLIAM BLACKWOOD AND SONS,
EDINBURGH AND LONDON.
M.DCCC.XLVI.

CONTENTS.

INTRODUCTION. . . . . P i

CHAPTER I.

Early life of Elspath Simpson—Her union with Robert Buchan—Indications of her becoming a wild visionary—The Rev. Hugh White of Irvine dismissed from the ministry for embracing her dogmas—He becomes a field preacher, and his attendants are henceforth called "Buchanites"—The people of Irvine maltreat Luckie Buchan for having bewitched the minister—She retires to Perthshire, where she is joined by White and a few followers — He proclaims her to be the woman mentioned in the Revelation of St John—Their impious whimsies rejected by the people of Muthill—They are compelled to leave that place—They return to Irvine, but are also banished thence. . . . . P 1

CHAPTER II.

The Buchanites' journey to Nithsdale—Their habitation, and unrestrained manner of living there described—An armed crowd assemble at night to drive them out of that locality—Luckie Buchan and White escape the fury of the mob, but are again assailed at the Manse of Wamphray—Mrs Buchan's epistolary correspondence—Divine Dictionary—Extracts from that singular work—Blasphemous pretensions of Mother Buchan—The destruction of the world circumstantially described. . . . . P 60

CONTENTS.

CHAPTER III.

The Buchanites imposed on by a dissolute officer of the Royal Marines—Andrew Innes, when on a mission into England, suddenly called home, with his converts, to meet the Lord in the clouds—The midnight manifestation at New Cample—The great fast of forty days commenced—Several of those engaged in that wild project nearly starved to death—The fasting scheme interrupted by the interference of the county magistrates—The Buchanites suspected of the crime of infanticide—Andrew Innes dismissed from the society—His vision at Leadhills—Mother Buchan attempts again to scale the sky—Circumstances connected with that ridiculous affair. . P. 95

CHAPTER IV.

Many of the disappointed expectants of immortality become disaffected—Luckie and her coadjutor committed to prison—Subsequently tried by the kirk-session of Closeburn for criminal conversation—Retrospective account of Andrew Innes—He returns with his wife and infant daughter to the Society—The Buchanites banished from Dumfries-shire—Their arrival and residence at Tarbreach, in Galloway—They remove to Auchengibbert, where they work for wages—Singular instance of their superstitious veneration for the founder of their sect—Credulous account of her culinary powers—Many of the members of the Society become disaffected and unruly—Mother Buchan complains of their backslidings—She is not allowed by Mr White to go from home, nor permitted to speak to strangers on religious topics—Her last illness—Commotion caused by her death—That she visibly ascended to heaven affirmed by those who watched her corpse by night—The place of her interment consequently concealed—Parallel between her and Mother Lee. . . . . P. 133

CHAPTER V.

Mr White publicly recants all he has advanced respecting the divine mission of Mrs Buchan—Those of the Society who entertain a similar opinion proceed with him to America—Account of them in the New World—Jean Gardner, the person referred to by Burns in his epistle to David Siller—The true Buchanites remove to Larghill, a wild moorland farm—They continue to hold the "faith and practice" inculcated by their founder—They subsequently remove to Crocketford, where, as they die, they are buried in the kail-yard—Anecdotes of some of the members who died there—The Buchanite dwelling-house at Crocketford described—Peculiarities of its inmates at the time my correspondence commenced with Andrew Innes, the last of the sect—Multiplicity and bent of his writings—His fanciful intercourse with the shade of Mrs Buchan, as my errand boy—His extraordinary conduct on hearing that I had discovered the first temporary burial-place of Mrs Buchan—The time of the expected advent of Mrs Buchan passes without altering his faith—His death, and interment with the remains of Mrs Buchan . . . . P. 178

APPENDIX . . . . . . P 239

THE BUCHANITES.

INTRODUCTION.

FEW females have acted such an extraordinary part on the stage of life, as Mrs Buchan. She gave herself out to be the Third Person in the Godhead,[1] and pretended to confer immortality on whomsoever she breathed; and promised, eventually, to translate, direct to heaven in a body, without their tasting death, all who put unlimited faith in her divine mission. She also personified the Woman described in the Revelation of St John, as being clothed with the Sun and the Moon; and pretended to have brought forth the Man-child who was to rule all nations with a rod of iron,[2] in the person of the Reverend Hugh White, Minister of the Relief congregation of Irvine.

[1] See White's Divine Dictionary, printed at Dumfries in the year 1785.
[2] Revelations, xii 1.

Extravagant and blasphemous as these pretensions were, Our Lady found adherents even among the descendants of the pious Covenanters of the Lowlands of Scotland, who, renouncing every compact by which mankind is distinguished from the brute creation, left their homes and their relations to follow her, in the delusive hope of escaping the common lot of humanity.

From the name of the founder, these enthusiasts were called Buchanites. At the time they appeared in Ayrshire, the belief in witchcraft not being totally eradicated from the minds of the people, the singular tenets of this sect were attributed to the influence of demoniac agency, rather than to distempered organisation. Mrs Buchan was supposed to possess such a proficiency in the *black art*, as to cause any person on whom she laid her hand, instantly to forget all earthly concerns, and follow her, though it were " to the utmost limits of the earth," with the most implicit devotion. But, so far as I have been able to obtain a knowledge of Mrs Buchan's acquirements, it was chiefly by a wonderful volubility of tongue, well directed to the object she had in view, that she succeeded in seducing the unwary.

History abounds with instances of the extravagant

pretensions of impostors who arrogated to themselves prophetic powers, and who succeeded in prevailing on the weak and ignorant to believe their pretended revelations and heavenly missions. My intention is not merely to add another to the list of these hypocrites, or victims of self-delusion, but also to show another instance of the folly of departing from sound reason and common sense in matters of religion, by bringing under the reader's view an epitome of the *Faith and Practice* of the Buchanites: the former, differing from all the established points of the Christian faith, and the latter, from many of the general usages of civilised society.

While the voices of the Great Man Child and his abettors, were heard fervently imploring all who would be saved from sin and death, to rally round the Light of God, as seen shining in the person of Mrs Buchan, some of the periodical works of the day published, occasionally, incidental notices of the progress of the Buchanites. The contents of these articles have been carefully collated with the verbal accounts and written communications of several respectable individuals who were personally acquainted with Luckie Buchan, the soubriquet by which she was known in Galloway, and who have kindly rendered me all the information in their power on this subject. Among these, I cannot here deny myself the satisfaction of mentioning the respectable names of the Rev. John Richmond, minister of Southdean, in Roxburghshire, son of Dr Richmond, who was minister of Irvine when Mrs Buchan and her followers were compelled to leave that town; also of William Ayton, Esq. of Hamilton, the author of many celebrated works on agricultural subjects, and lately of a pamphlet on the state of the Scotch Church; of Mrs Major Skirving of Croys, daughter of the late Rev. Dr Muirhead, minister of Urr when the Buchanites lived at Auchengibbert; and of Dr Mundell, rector of Wallace Hall Academy, in Dumfries-shire. To Francis Laurie, Esq. of Tinwald Shaws, Dumfries-shire, I am indebted for the reminiscences of his aunt, Mrs Black, who is yet alive (1841), respecting the manners and customs of the Buchanites, with some of whom she was personally acquainted while they remained at New Cample; to Colonel James Gordon of Culvennan I am much indebted for information respecting the first temporary burial-place of Mrs Buchan; to Mr Thomas Bradley of Wolviston, in the county of Durham, for his kindness in placing in my hands several important original documents relating to his father's connexion with the

Buchanites, and for his own reminiscences of that singular sect; and to the Rev. William Lindsay, minister of the Relief congregation of Dowhill, clerk of the Relief presbytery of Glasgow, for examining and extracting from the records of the Relief church, in his possession, several important particulars respecting Mr White; but I am chiefly indebted to Mr Andrew Innes of Crocketford, without whose assistance the materials I had collected respecting the Buchanites would, it is probable, never have appeared before the public.

Andrew Innes was born at Muthill, in Perthshire, in July 1757, of parents belonging to the cottar class; and after receiving the education common to his class in those times, was bred to the profession of a carpenter, and he has at times, in his later years, been heard to allude, with apparent complacency, to that having also been the profession of the LORD!—on so low and familiar a level was it the character of his singularly constructed mind, to place at point of view even the highest and most sacred mystical things! He became acquainted with Mrs Buchan in 1783, and then formed an unalienable attachment to her person and pretensions. His exertions contributed much to the forming of the Buchanite Society of 1784, of which community he remained an effective member to the last, and, in right of survivorship, has become possessed of all the property that pertained to that body. This put it in his power to place at my disposal all the books and writings which had thus fallen into his hands; and he has done this in the most obliging manner. In addition to this, he has drawn up for my information an account of the proceedings of the Buchanites, in which he was either personally concerned, or which came under his observation, from their commencement as a society to the present time. Some of the topics therein narrated, are alluded to in the following letter:—

" Crocketford, 28th January 1839.

" My Dear Friend,

"Your kindness has completely overwhelmed me with wonder. If there is any thing in the narrative not explained to your satisfaction, I am quite willing to do so, or to give you any paper in my possession. I expect the perusal of the Divine Dictionary has settled your mind as to the accusation of witchcraft against the founder of our society, or of our having gained any worldly benefit by disposing of our effects, and forming a separate society where all things were common. The account which I have given you in the narrative, will show you, that the real cause of our leaving settled habitations and becoming outcasts of society, and a common reproach to the world, was the confident hope of being speedily translated to heaven without tasting death.[1]

" You will not, perhaps, easily perceive the cause of Mr White's publishing to the world, that the author of his spiritual knowledge and spiritual light, was the woman seen in heaven, nor the reason of our fasting for forty days at Closeburn. It may, however, be proper for me to mention here, that there are several circumstances connected with the fast omitted in the narrative, because they could not be comprehended or believed by any person who was not there at the time. You will not, perhaps, understand the cause of our no longer working gratis to our neighbours after the fast—or why Mr White made such a complete change of writing and preaching at Auchengibbert. These things, I think, will require a few explanatory notes, and I will make them out for you in the course of a few weeks.

[1] 1 Thessalonians, iv. 15, 16, 17

"You know that, 'Friend Mother in the Lord,' was the name given by us to the founder of our society; and it is only when conversing with strangers who do not know her by that name, that I call her Mrs Buchan. Her letters contained in the book now in your possession, were all copied by me after her death. Her address to any of her family was always 'my child,' to strangers 'dear,'—so often repeated, that I have omitted many of them in the same letter; and, when speaking of divine things, 'O! O! O!' She repeated O! so frequently, that I have omitted some of them in copying also, which I now mention to my shame.[1]

"I mentioned, in my first letter to you, that I had no desire that any of Mr White's writings should be sent to the public, but, upon further consideration, I leave it altogether to your own choice to publish whatever you please concerning the society. As I have given you a just statement of facts, I have no reason to fear being contradicted; and though, like Elijah of old, disappointed in faith, I rejoice in being the first and only individual on earth who has had any inclination

[1] Mr Innes, at my request, wrote an Introduction to the MS. volume of Mrs Buchan's letters, with a long explanatory note to each letter. These will be frequently alluded to in the course of the following sketch.

to tell the truth of the author of our society. What I have written to you, may appear as unlikely as the resurrection of Jesus, after his body had been mangled, and his heart pierced with a spear. But I hope the time is not far distant, when you will obtain a proof, as substantial as Thomas did, of the truth of what I have just stated.

"If, upon further consideration, I find I have omitted any thing in the narrative which I think might be interesting to you, I will write it down—for I am your sincere friend and well-wisher,

"Andrew Innes."

In the course of the following sketch, I have quoted such passages from the correspondence of Mrs Buchan and from the writings of Mr Innes, as tend most to place, in their own words, the dogmas and practices of the sect before the reader, that he may be thereby the better enabled to form his own judgment on the faith and practice of the Buchanites.

The clerical character of Mrs Buchan's coadjutor, is thus given by a modern writer. "In the year 1781, the Rev. Hugh White, a native of the parish of St Ninian's, and a licentiate of the Church of Scotland, was received into connexion with the Relief Synod.

He was speedily called and ordained to the pastorate of the Relief church, Irvine. The settlement was harmonious; and though his talents and acquirements were not of the first order, he was pretty much esteemed as a preacher. He delighted, however, rather to speak from Sinai than from Zion. Like men of this stamp, he was vain of his own attainments, while he was denouncing others with the terrors of the law. Being easily puffed up, he suffered himself to be cajoled and drawn aside by the flattery of Mrs Buchan, an artful fanatic, and thus gained to himself a notoriety, which his slender talents in the ordinary discharge of duty, would never have won; but which, after all, was rather a matter of humiliation than of honour.'[1]

[1] Struthers' Hist. of the Relief Church, p. 335; Glasgow, 1843. Christian Journal, for January 1835, p. 9.

CHAPTER I.

Early Life of Elspath Simpson—Her union with Robert Buchan—Indications of her becoming a wild visionary—The Reverend Hugh White of Irvine dismissed from the ministry for embracing her dogmas—He becomes a field-preacher, and his attendants are henceforth called "Buchanites"—The people of Irvine maltreat Luckie Buchan for having bewitched the minister—She retires to Perthshire, where she is joined by White and a few followers—He proclaims her to be the Woman mentioned in the Revelation of St John—Their impious whimsies rejected by the people of Muthill—They are compelled to leave that place—They return to Irvine, but are also banished thence.

Mrs Buchan was the daughter of John Simpson and Margaret Gordon, who kept a small way-side public house on the old road between Banff and Portsoy, at a place called Fatmacken, where she was born about the year 1738, and was named Elspath; but ere the child had completed her third year, her mother died, and her father having married again shortly afterwards, she was sent into a strange family, whose circumstances were in such a hampered state, that her bedding consisted of a bag stuffed with straw laid down on the ground beside the fire at night, with an empty sack for a coverlet, which were removed in the morning, and stowed away till required again in the evening.[1] During the day she

---

[1] Mrs Buchan's letter to the Reverend Francis Okely of Northampton, (Buchanites' Letter-book, p. 87. Innes's MS. p 126.) Mr Okely

was employed herding her master's cows. How long she remained at service does not appear, but if her own words may be relied on, she was not such a person as most people would wish to employ. " I had no pleasure in working, and ever forgot the directions given me ; so that I learned more by the eye than the ear." She was, however, at length taken into the employment of a distant relation of her mother's, after whom she had been named Elspath, and was by her taught to sew and read. This young woman had been recently married to a West India planter, a native of Banffshire, and was about to proceed with her husband to his possessions in Jamaica. Young Elspath, for the purpose of accompanying them thither, proceeded with them to Greenock, but while waiting there for a vessel to take them to their final destination, she left her friends to associate with idle company, and appears then to have contracted those depraved habits which she afterwards inculcated respecting matrimony.

According to a contemporary writer, she trepanned, at Ayr, a working potter named Robert Buchan, to be her husband;[1] but if the union was legally solemnized, it does not appear in any of the registers of the parish of Ayr.[2] Buchan, becoming ashamed

---

translated Engelbrecht's Divine Visions of Hell and Heaven; New Heaven and New Earth; Mountain of Salvation, and Three States—Ecclesiastical, Political, and Economical; with a Life of Engelbrecht which was printed at Northampton in 1780, in one vol. 12mo.

[1] Account of the Buchanites, by Henry M'Dowal, published in 1792.

[2] "I have made a search in the registers of marriages of the town and parish of Ayr, from 1740 to 1780, for the marriage of Robert

of her licentious conduct at Ayr, removed with her to Banff, and there commenced a manufactory of earthenware on his own account; but that undertaking not succeeding to the extent of his wishes, he proceeded to Glasgow in search of employment, leaving his wife, with one son and two daughters, at Banff, " to provide for themselves as they best could,"[1] by keeping a school for teaching children to sew, and, Mr Innes thinks, to read also, although very ill qualified for such an undertaking. She might, however, have made a comfortable livelihood, had not her other and stronger propensities interfered with the sedate carriage necessary to the success of a schoolmistress. She seems to have neglected both her family and school to carry out the details of a divine apocalypse, charging her with a heavenly mission, a part of which she thus describes:—

"To inform you how far I went, and how many opinions I tried, seeking the way of truth, is more than I can do on paper; but I may say that I went from sea to sea seeking the Word of the Lord, but could not find it.

Buchan and Elspath Simpson, but it does not appear in any of these years (Signed) WILLIAM M'DERMIT, Senior Clerk."

[1] Society's MSS p 147—"Robert Buchan and Elspet Simson had many children, but only three of them were alive when she left her husband—a son, who continued with his father, and two daughters—one of them about nineteen and the other about twenty-one years of age, who imbibed their mother's notions, and accompanied her"—Christian Journal for January 1835, p. 10. It appears that the son joined the Buchanite society also, as will be seen in a subsequent part of this work

"In the year 1774, the power of God wrought such a wonderful change on my senses, that I overcame the flesh so as not to make use of earthly food for some weeks, which made all that saw me conclude that I was going to depart this life, and many came to hear me speak, which was all about God's love to mortals. . . . Had there been a gallows erected at every door where I had an opportunity of speaking of Christ, or of hearing him spoken of, I would not have stayed from going there; and the more any sought to keep me back, it only tended the more to stir me up to run the faster." [1]

Mrs Buchan was a regular attender at what were called "fellowship meetings." These were societies of persons who met weekly, for religious purposes; and although some of the clergymen in the neighbourhood were in the habit of attending, she was generally the principal disputant on religious subjects. Although her views of certain passages in Scripture differed widely from the opinions commonly entertained, she made several converts, the most enthusiastic of whom was the wife of Captain Cook, commander of the Prince of Wales revenue cutter, who was long known as one of the most active officers on the northern station. Mrs Buchan thus writes of that lady—"Mrs Cook and I spent many hours together, mourning for our own sins and for the sins of others; but Satan made use of her husband, a very irreligious and fiery-tempered man, to separate

[1] MS. Letter-book, p. 38.

us. He was, and still is, the captain of a king's cutter. He used every means to keep her from seeing me or writing to me; but a greater stroke was to follow. She took a fever, and they, hearing her speak of nothing but Christ and the other world, and calling continually for me, concluded that I had put her mad with religion, and she was kept in a dark room for three weeks. But all the means they used, tended only to increase her disorder; and it noised about that the captain intended to take my life."[1]

The clergy now became Mrs Buchan's inveterate enemies, and were chiefly instrumental in raising the populace against her doctrines; but "her manner of life was most offensive to those with whom she was connected."[2]

Her school being deserted, and finding her life in imminent danger in her native county, acting under the advice of her friends, she removed, with her children, to Glasgow, where she arrived in March 1781, and was cordially received by her husband,[3] who was then employed in a pottery in that city.

Being fond of epistolary correspondence, she continued to write frequently to the members of "fellowship societies" at Banff, for a considerable time after her arrival in Glasgow; but an unfavourable report regarding her mode of life, reached her native place. Receiving a communication on that subject

[1] Letter-book, p. 28. [2] Note by Mr Innes, p. 147.
[3] MS Letter book, p. 32.

from a friend there, wishing her to change her mode of life, she replied—"The things that have been said among you, grieve my very soul. I am sorry you give yourself so much trouble concerning my family, for fear I have too few of my thoughts in the world; but I thank God for supporting me. I employ my hands as well as ever. I cannot conceal the goodness of the Lord, who has turned the evil intentions of my enemies to my good."[1] To another friend she writes thus on the same subject—"I spent day and night pleading for them at the throne of grace. But, for my love to them, they became foes to me; and I do believe some of them never prayed more earnestly in their lives, than that God would take me out of their way; which prayer they got answered, for the Lord called on me by his providence, and made me willing to go. I will write to some of them, although I know they hate me, which I do not wonder at. I was dead to them, and they wanted me buried out of their sight."[2]

Mr Hugh White, minister of the Relief congregation of Irvine, in Ayrshire,[3] was at this time the most

---

[1] MS Letter-book, p. 3.

[2] Ibid, p. 12.

[3] "Mr White succeeded Mr Jack, as minister of the Relief congregation of Irvine, and was ordained 3d July 1782. Though he was popular at Irvine, his childish eagerness after doctrinal novelty made him be regarded, in expounding the oracle of God, 'as a very unsafe guide' As a preacher he was described in homely but expressive terms, 'a coarse hewer'"—Christian Journal, vol v p. 306. This shows that he had been only settled in his charge as minister at Irvine about nine months, when he became acquainted with Mrs Buchan

popular preacher of his sect in the west of Scotland. Mrs Buchan having heard his piety much spoken of, wished very much to hear him preach, and an opportunity soon occurred of gratifying her curiosity in that respect. Mr White being called to assist at a sacrament in the neighbourhood of Glasgow, in December 1782, she attended on that occasion; and, being captivated with his oratory, she communicated the flattering account by letter, of his being the first minister who had spoken effectually to her heart.

"Glasgow, 17th January 1783.

"Rev. and Dear Sir—Whom I love in our sweet Lord Jesus Christ—I write you as a friend, not after the flesh, nor according to the flesh, but as a child of another family, that has lain in the womb of the everlasting decree from all eternity—a promised seed actually born from above. . . . . . I have met with many disappointments from ministers, who were neither strangers nor pilgrims on earth, and I can say, by sad experience, that I have been more stumbled and grieved by ministers, than by all the men in the world, or by all the devils in hell; but I have rejoiced many times, by the eye of faith, to see you, before I saw you with the eyes of my body. On Saturday night, when your discourse was ended, an acquaintance says to me, 'What do you think of Mr White?'—I answered, 'What do you think of Jesus Christ? for I have lost sight of the minister and of myself.' . . . .

"When I think on those words which Christ said

—' I am the door!' O, blessed door, which Sin nor his elder brother Satan cannot shut, for it will still be open to the heirs of glory! and methinks I have often rapped at the door with my little hand of faith, and was heard and answered. I will not say I got the very thing I asked, for *bairns* know not always what is best for them; but the Lord never sent me away without alms; and he is never weary of me, although I am ever fashing him. . . . .

"Though I have been a gazing-stock to the world, and an eye-sore to the devil these five years, I have lost nothing, for my Lord has been at much pains to learn me to put no confidence in the world. . . . .

"From your friend and sister in Christ,
    (Signed)   "ELSPATH SIMPSON.

"The Rev. Hugh White, Irvine." [1]

It was just at this period that Andrew Innes became acquainted with Mrs Buchan, in the following accidental manner:—"In March 1783," says Andrew, "I went from Muthill, in Perthshire, to Glasgow, to attend the sacrament, and lodged with my old landlady, in Dowhill. On Saturday morning, a little before the church bells began to ring, while I was employed dressing in the closet, I heard a female voice in the kitchen, conversing with the mistress, and the subject was concerning King Hezekiah showing the treasures of the Lord's house to

[1] MS Letter-book, page 1

the servants of the King; this she continued till the bells were nearly done ringing, when she accompanied us to the door of the Relief church, leading a blind woman all the way. The person who seemed to be so well acquainted with the Scriptures, was Mrs Buchan, who afterwards became the founder of the sect that bore her name. I had never even heard of her name before, but my old landlady informed me that she had been acquainted with her for some time, and had often heard of her extensive correspondence with ministers and other people on religious subjects; and that many religious people were in the habit of visiting her.

"After service, she attended us back to our quarters at Dowhill, and, after dinner, invited me to her lodgings, which were then in the upper flat of an old wooden house in the Saltmarket, and were but poorly furnished.[1] As soon as I went in, she rose and conducted me to Glasgow Green, where she laid open to my view how the kings and priests of Israel became a curse to the people, and how David, by his adultery with Bathsheba, occasioned the death of so many people, with other parts of Scripture which I knew to be truths so simple and easy to be comprehended, that I wondered I had never seen them before in the same light. We parted in the evening, and I called, by appointment, again at her house on Monday

---

[1] " Robert Buchan, her husband, was then a workman at the Delf-work, at the Broomielaw "—Struthers' History of the Relief Church of Scotland: Glasgow edition, 1843, p 335. Christian Journal for Jan 1835, p 10.

before leaving town, for the purpose of seeing her letters of correspondence, which were chiefly with ministers of various sects in Banff and Aberdeenshire; but at that time Mr White, the Relief minister at Irvine, was her only one."

Mr White had shown the communication which he had received from Mrs Buchan, to several of his sect, who were so highly pleased with her religious views, that they wished to become personally acquainted with her. Mr White, accordingly, invited her to Irvine, where she arrived in 1783, and became his lodger. The whole sect gave her a very welcome reception; and Mr White, to afford them an opportunity of hearing her speak on sacred scripture, appointed a day for examining part of his congregation in the church. "He made the dark or mystical parts of her letters the questions to be answered, and when this was not done distinctly, he either explained the meaning himself, or applied to her to do so; and she was always ready to assist either party; and she did so in a manner that surprised all her hearers."

From her heavenly conversation and extraordinary gifts, they soon began to consider her as a valuable acquisition to their party. Religion was the constant topic of her conversation. In every company, and on all occasions, she introduced it. Her time was wholly employed in visiting from house to house, in praying and solving doubts, answering questions, and in expounding the Scriptures.

Some of the congregation at length began to

entertain doubts of the orthodoxy of her principles, all of which had been imbibed by their minister; they consequently expressed their dissatisfaction at his ministry, and desired him to dismiss her as a dangerous person.[1] In a few weeks afterwards she left Irvine, but, before her departure, wrote Mr White as follows:—

To the Rev. Hugh White, Irvine.

Irvine, April 1783.

" My dear Child,

" The Lord's way with you has been like himself, wonderful: He may say, Hugh White, you have not chosen me, but I have chosen you. Hugh White, I have been a witness concerning you of what has been written of Jeremiah—that he was sanctified in the womb. God, your Heavenly Father, knoweth my birth-pains of heavenly love have been far surpassing the love of woman; but, oh come and behold a wonder now, I am bigger than ever! God, for Christ's sake, will keep me pregnant with his own glory and your everlasting happiness, till that thrice-happy day when those who sow in tears shall reap in joy. . . . .
O! O! O! for thy great name's sake, seal home on the heart of Hugh White that most holy admonition with everlasting life and power, 'Be thou faithful unto the death, and I will give you a crown of life.' The Lord now comforts my soul with these words— 'My servant deals prudently, and shall be very high in righteousness.' Arise, my child! this mantle belong-

[1] Sir John Sinclair's Statistical Account, vol. vii pp. 181, 182, 183

eth unto thee—we also shall be with thee. Be of good faith, and do it,—there shall be a performance of all that is promised. Now my dearly beloved, I hope you will let no person see this while you live, if you can help it, but keep it as a pledge of love, not from me, but from your God and my God, whose will is even your sanctification. I believe in the strength of your faith, the increase of your hope, the inflammation of your love. May the joy of the Lord be your strength, and may his strength be your joy! This is the believing prayer and hearty desire of her who loves you, and all that concerns you, next to my Lord and your Lord. I am confident he has begun the good work in you, and that you will continue it till the day of Jesus Christ. Amen. (Signed) ELSPATH SIMPSON."[1]

Although Mr White had not then declared Mrs Buchan to be really the woman prophesied in the Revelation of St John, yet he boldly affirmed her to be a saint of no ordinary description, and the harbinger of a light that would unveil the darkness of Antichrist, that had long overshadowed the land. This delusion, with the blasphemous opinions he had imbibed from her, were so very offensive to many of his congregation, that they gave him fully to understand, that, if he persisted in these heterodox opinions,

[1] MS. Letter-book, p 65 Note by Mr Innes —"This letter was written in Mr White's own house, during the time of her first visit, was found among other papers left by Mr White when he went to America, and was copied into this book for the purpose of being preserved."—P. 151.

a formal charge would be made against him to the presbytery, for propagating doctrines so contrary to the Confession of Faith. But notwithstanding every remonstrance that could be made with him on the subject, he continued to advocate most strenuously the soundness of the faith he had recently adopted.[1]

A paper was accordingly drawn up by the persons who opposed his new doctrines, containing what they supposed to be her principles; and he was desired to declare if such were his principles also. He acknowledged they were, and readily subscribed them as such.

An account of these proceedings was, without loss of time, forwarded by Mr White to his idol, Mrs Buchan; but this letter, as well as others from him to the same person,[2] being lost, we give the purport

[1] "The leading persons of his congregation, being dissatisfied with his doctrine, at length sent a deputation to him, earnestly entreating him to dismiss Mrs Buchan; but he was so enamoured of her mystic views, that he declared he would sooner cut off his right arm. But they need put themselves to no trouble, for if the majority of his church was dissatisfied he would go away."—Irvine Relief Session Minutes.

[2] It appears from a letter from Mrs Buchan to the Rev. Francis Okely of Northampton, that she carried on a weekly correspondence with Mr White for four months before she became personally acquainted with him; but, unfortunately, all his letters to her appear to be irrecoverably lost, which is thus accounted for by Mr Innes:—

"When our Friend Mother came to Irvine, she brought with her a little hand-trunk filled with letters from various ministers and religious societies in the north of England, and with many from Mr White. Although our departure from various places was sudden and unexpected, she managed to preserve the little hand-trunk, with its contents, till we came to Auchengibbert. She then evidently became more careless about her letters; and whilst she was with us, we never minded them. Many of Mr White's letters lay among the papers of

of it as related by Mr Innes:—" He informed her by letter of the opposition he had met with among the members of his congregation, after he had left Irvine; stating the truths they had attempted to condemn, and how he had confuted them with ease —equal to John Knox when contending with Papists —and how he saw the world at that day involved in darkness, nothing inferior to Popery, and that he thought his clerical brethren would quit a wrong cause as soon as it was laid before them how mistaken they had been—a thing he had little doubt of being able to perform."

Possessed of little worldly experience, and feeling merely as a young Christian, that he had no desire to reject a conviction of truth, Mr White seems to have supposed that all others would act under a similar feeling, and that his enemies would yield and join his standard as they did that of John Knox. But he did not see how far his situation differed from that of the Scottish Reformer. John Knox opposed Popery with a true description of its evils, but he did not do so single-handed: all the disaffected barons of Scotland were ready to join him, and, like the barons of Germany and England, to grasp at the wealth of the Popish clergy, that they might add the lands of the Catholic church to their own. If Mr White, therefore, expected a victory such as was

the society, in my drawers, till the year 1836, when, being very ill of the influenza, and not expecting to recover, I burned them all, to save my executors trouble, with many other documents which I now find would have been highly prized by you"

gained by John Knox, he wanted all the assistance of the barons and their dependants; and his brother clergy being sufficiently aware of this, paid little attention to his exposition of their errors, while they knew their income was safe.

Although Mrs Buchan knew well, from experience, the opposition he was likely to meet with, yet, in her answer to his letter, she does not discourage his young faith, but makes him acquainted with her joy at finding one so full of courage.

"Glasgow, 23d May 1783

"My dearly beloved Brother in our loving Lord Jesus,—I have received your most agreeable letter, and I warrantably believe that you will grow a great man with your living Lord and lawgiver, Jesus Christ. How happy I am to see, to hear, and to read your *Me* and *My*—it is the language of the faith of God's elect. It is known to him who knows all things, that there is nothing on this side of death and judgment that could give me greater joy, than seeing, hearing, and believing, that Mr Hugh White is a bold soldier, fighting under the banner of King Jesus. Oh how my soul, and all that in me is, rejoices at your having been born from above, and that your lot and my lot has been cast in the same land! I hope you can say, by experience, My love is mine, and I am his—he feeds me among the lilies till the day breaks and the shadows fly away. The shadows are fled away, and the true light has come at last; the day-spring from on high hath visited us, and the day-star hath risen in our hearts—and happy are they who are alive to God.

"But, my dear, let me chide you in love for writing me such short letters. You did not write any thing about *Bell* and the dear child.[1] I have received several letters this week from various individuals of the flock of which the Holy Ghost has made you overseer; and I cannot but comfort you with this—that I think the Lord is blessing your labour of love. *A minister that has access to God* by faith and by the spirit, is a greater blessing than many are sensible of. O happy are the people that hear the joyful sound and know it—they shall enter by the gates into the eternal city! Some of your people have refreshed my soul with the glad tidings that have been amongst you for these two Sabbaths. You will never find Christ worse than he has been—he will do still better to you than at the beginning. . . . . How can they desire to leave this world, who know nothing of another world but by hearsay—such persons know nothing of Christ. I wonder how the professors of this age pretend to know God, when they do not keep his commandments. . . . . Old things are done away with, and all things are become new—all that is mine is thine. So no more at present from your loving sister in the Lord.

(Signed) "ELSPATH SIMPSON.

"To the Rev. Hugh White, Irvine"

[1] Mrs White, and a child which she had during the time that Mrs B. visited her.

Mr Innes was informed of the opposition raised against Mr White in Irvine, and that he was to be tried by the presbytery, for heresy, at Glasgow—at which trial it appears Mrs Buchan wished Mr Innes to be present.

"Glasgow, 17th June 1783

"My very dear Friend,

"I received a very few lines from you under cover, with a letter to deliver to Mr Pitcairn at the college. I was disappointed at my name not being even mentioned in Mr Pitcairn's letter. I would not have served you so—God is my witness. But I do not write to give you trouble—for your sorrow is my sorrow, and your joy is my joy; but if you knew how much you are on my mind, you would have wrote me another kind of a letter. You are not only on my spirit before the Lord, but you are carried in the arms of my godly friends in Irvine, who are rapidly growing in grace and in the knowledge of Jesus Christ. My desire of seeing you is much increased. Mr Stewart of Anderston will have his communion at the usual time, at which there will be some of my acquaintances from Irvine; and they have written me, that they would be happy to see you; and, indeed, I think it would be for your advantage to come. Let me know, by post, if you resolve on coming.

"My dear, I wish to be plain with you. There are several things in John Pitcairn's letter from you, which I did not like, and could not approve of. I would ask you one question:—Did there ever any grace grow in the garden of corrupt nature? Surely not. . . . . The dead and the living have no communication together; and this I can say by experience, for if my life and conversation be as disagreeable to the world as theirs is to me, no wonder they are weary of me. I thank God that the act of his justification freed me from the condemning power of sin, and the act of adoption freed me from the state of sin—they that are born of God, cannot sin. I am a living witness to that precious truth; but I have no more hand in my sanctification, than I have in my justification or adoption. If I could be taken up above the sun of this world, and, when looking down, was asked what I saw, I would answer—I saw this pit of sin and corruption in which we now live, and in which Jesus died, that I might be delivered from the bondage of corruption upon honourable terms. . . . .

"My dear, I hope you will consider these things. I cannot write so full about them as I would like to do, I have so little time. This is the eighth letter I have answered this week, and it is only Thursday yet. I write the most of my letters in thenight-time, for I cannot bear any disturbance. I recommend you to God—pray for Jerusalem—pray for your loving sister in Christ—ELSPATH SIMPSON.[1]

"To Mr Andrew Innes."

Mr Innes was so proud of this letter, that he shewed it to all his acquaintances; and, notwithstand-

[1] MS Letter-book, pp 47, 48, 49, 50.

ing the most strenuous remonstrances on the part of his friends and relations, he resolved to proceed to Glasgow at the time appointed, of which he apprised Mrs Buchan by post. To this communication she alludes, in the following letter to Mrs White:—

"Glasgow, June 1783.

"Dearest of Sisters,

"You have a goodly heritage, a large charter, and good security for it. You have God your father-in-law, and your everlasting husband Jesus Christ. He has given you a back-bond signed and sealed with his own blood. Your privileges are great, and your benefits many—yea, the Lord will be better and better to you every day. . . . .

"The Lord wants, above all things, that we would live at his royal expense—he is a liberal landlord—a bountiful giver. Let us walk fast—for we walk by faith, not by sight. Though we should be led in the dark, as to our lot in Providence let us not fear, for the government is upon the shoulders of King Jesus, and the key is at his side, upon his golden girdle. Believe me, my dear love, there is nothing in glory, grace, or providence, but what is on your side. Although hell and earth, men and devils, be raging against us, they can only rage on their own ground, and cannot harm us. . . . .

"Tell my dear sister, Mrs Hunter, that her letter had no fault but one—it was too short; but I hope her next will be longer. Let humble holy Magdaline know that I long to see her. I daresay the devil has no memory of me in Irvine—he has enough to do there without me—let him rage on—his time is now short; but he is up in other places also—and the people are so blind and ignorant, that they lay the blame to my charge—so that you need not be surprised although you should hear of my being brought to trial for turning the world upside down.

"I have sent you another, which I received from Andrew Innes, to let you see how the devil, in flesh and blood, is up in arms against him. I beg your sympathy in faith and love towards him, and put others in mind of it also—Yours for ever in the Lord, ELSPATH SIMPSON."

On the morning of the trial, Mrs Buchan thus writes to the Rev. Hugh White:—

"Glasgow, 28th June 1783

"MY VERY DEAR BROTHER IN THE LORD JESUS CHRIST,—With what pleasure do I think of you and write to you, whom the whole Trinity has loved with an everlasting love. You are on the Lord's side, therefore the enemies of the Lord are up in arms against you; but go you forward, fear not, for the *Breaker* is come up before them. . . . . You are now looking so high to Jesus, that you are out of sight of yourself; and it matters not though your soul and body never have any communion with self. I am here like a pelican in the wilderness. The people are as much afraid of me as if I had the plague, or as if I would rob them of life.

"Believe me, it is exceedingly joyful to me to see the fruits of my prayers of faith in you, and the effects of your labour of love. Whatever thou shalt ask in my name, thou shalt receive it. The great *I am* will keep you like the apple of his eye.—Your sister in Christ, ELSPATH SIMPSON."[1]

Mr White's real friends saw his situation at this time, in quite a different light from the frenzied view taken of it by Mrs Buchan. He was a native of Stirlingshire, had been professor of logic in an American college, and was accounted a most profound theologian. His fame as a preacher of the gospel was known in this country, and on the death of Mr Jack, first minister of the Relief congregation in Irvine, he received a "call" from that body to be pastor, which he accepted. After the commencement of his acquantance with Mrs Buchan, her marvels appear to have overthrown, as if by magic, all his former erudition, and to have turned his thoughts into another channel.[2] To account for this sudden change in the opinions and deportment of Mr White, the populace supposed that Luckie Buchan was skilled in the "black art," and that she was in union and communion with the devil.

At the period of his trial, Mr White had a young wife and two children, one only three months, and

[1] MS Letter-book, pp. 50, 51.
[2] Forsyth's Beauties of Scotland, Edin. 1805, vol ii, pp 510 519
[3] MS Diary, p. 168.

the other not more than two years old. These considerations induced many persons interested in his welfare, to expostulate on the troubles and hardships to which he might expose himself and his family, by continuing to support dogmas which had never been recognised by any Christian community. But he heard them as if he heard them not—his trial proceeded—and his clerical brethren were obliged to eject him from his ministry.

However distressing this juncture in the life of Mr White might have been to his relations and friends, it was far otherwise to the crafty woman by whom he was so unaccountably misled.

The charges against Mr White were at length formally presented to the presbytery on 30th June 1783, but are not engrossed in the minutes. Mr White does not appear to have been present at that meeting of the presbytery, as Mrs Buchan writes him next day,—

"Glasgow, 1st July 1783

"MY BELOVED DEAR BROTHER IN AND NEAR TO OUR BELOVED LORD,—You are now appearing to be the child of another family—an heir of a kingdom that is not of this world—if you were of the world, the world would love its own; but because you are not of the world, the world hates you. I hope you know that your Holy Father will deal justly with men and with devils; he will let them put all their laws in force, and vent their malice, but it is not you they have engaged—though they vainly imagine so—it is no less than the whole powers of heaven they have presumed to engage. . . . .

"Many a love-letter has gone between you and me, but I bless our lovely Lord that the one dated yesterday is the sweetest in its nature that I ever received from you. I have been in more than ordinary heaviness to see so many at this time rushing against Jehovah's buckler. You are apprehended because you appear in strange apparel, but join me in praise and thanksgiving that they cannot strip you of any thing that you have from Christ—and, if they think you have any thing of theirs, they may try and take it from you and go their way—you can well spare it—having enough in the new covenant.

"You are born of the Spirit, and of blood, and of water. You resemble the son of a king, for a heroic spirit and a noble mind; and this is like to put your enemies distracted. Poor short-sighted creatures, they see nothing on the other side of death—they think that I have done all this—and many are praying that you had never seen me; but I am sure if they knew how happy I would be to spend my last breath and the last drop of my blood for Hugh White, they would not give themselves so much trouble. They say I am the most dangerous person that ever came to this place—they think they cannot live if I remain among them. They are like the Jews, they will not have the Saviour that is come, but they will have one that is to come. . . . .

"I am happy to think that you are so well prepared for this stroke; but it will do you no harm; for although the whole course of nature was set on fire, it would not singe one hair of your head. . . . It is no strange thing that has happened to you—fear not, your enemies are only strong on their own ground, and they have it only for a short time—they know nothing of your joy, and you know nothing of their sorrow; for, as you once wrote to me, 'When saints begin endless praises—sinners begin fruitless prayers.'

"Give my love in the Lord to Mr and Mrs Hunter;[1] may the Lord bless them, and cause his face to shine on them, and I firmly believe they shall have perfect peace. They are a great comfort to me, because I believe they are a great comfort to you. I have been greatly favoured by Magdaline's company, but I part with her that she may be a comfort to you, for I could carry your cross till you and I be within the gates of Heaven. I expect in kind Providence to see you soon, and therein I rejoice.

"Now unto him that loved us, and washed us from our sins in his own blood, be praise, and honour, and glory, from henceforth and for evermore, Amen.—Your loving sister in the Lord Jesus Christ, ELSPATH SIMPSON.

"To the Rev. Hugh White, Irvine.

"P.S.—I beg the favour of you, that the night you receive this letter, which will be on Thursday, that

[1] "I distinctly remember a gentleman of the name of Hunter, a writer in Irvine, who was one of Mrs Buchan's most devoted adherents."—Letter from the Rev John Richmond, minister of Southdean, in Roxburghshire. Mr Hunter was a slender, little, crooked-backed man.

you will read, in family worship, the 4th chapter of Jeremiah, and sing the 61st Psalm; and, if it be possible, begin exactly at ten o'clock; and in the joy of the Lord, although absent in body, I hope to join you; and when you come to the 19th verse, mind these words, "My bowels, my bowels! I am pained at my very heart. My heart maketh a noise in me. I cannot hold my peace, because thou hast heard, O my soul, the sound of the trumpet, the alarm of war." [1]

She wrote also, on 1st July, to Mrs White,—

"My beloved and very dear Sister,

"Your letter gave me joy and gladness—what a blessing it is that the love of God was shed abroad in your heart before the flood of enmity appeared! I hope you neither fear your enemies, nor fret against them as evil-doers: Fret not thyself unquietly, nor hatred bear to them that work iniquity, for even like unto the grass shall they soon be cut down. Set thou thy trust on the Lord, and be thou doing good, so thou shalt dwell upon the land, and verily shalt have food. My soul has good cause to rejoice in the Lord, at the agreeable news that your friends and mine gave of you. Fear nothing but God in love, and you shall have nothing else to fear. Now may the good-will of Him who dwelt in

[1] MS. Letter-book, pp. 55, 56, 57, 58, 59.

the bush, be with you and all that concerns you. Forget not me, for I cannot forget you and yours.

"ELSPATH SIMPSON."[1]

"A meeting of the presbytery was specially called on 8th July 1783, to consider the charges contained in the petition of the people of Irvine against Mr White; but, though it is mentioned that the sederunt was long, the minutes are certainly exceedingly short. The only thing I can gather from them is, that Mr White did not believe the Old Testament Saints to be the *Temples of the Spirit*—but the documents you refer to are not recorded. They would no doubt be preserved for a while by the clerk; but I think they must long ago have been destroyed."[2] This meeting was adjourned to the 8th August following, when the business was finally settled—Mr White having been found to entertain a number of sentiments contrary to Scripture, the sentence of suspension was unanimously carried against him.

Mr Innes, according to promise, visited Mrs Buchan at Glasgow, exactly at this time, and gives the following account of the proceedings against Mr

---

[1] MS. Letter-book, p. 63.

[2] Letter from the Rev. William Lindsay, dated 8th February 1840. "From the terms of the libel against Mr White, we learn that, by him, and, as we infer, by her, it was held, *first*, that sin does not adhere to the believer; *secondly*, that Christ tasted death for all men; and *thirdly*, that whilst the bodies of saints, under the New Testament, are the temples of the Holy Ghost, the saints, under the Old Testament, were not favoured with this distinction."—Statistical Account of Scotland: Irvine, Ayrshire. Edition 1842.

White:—"I called at Mrs Buchan's lodgings in the Saltmarket, but found her apartment so crowded with people from Irvine, that for a short time I could scarcely get so near her as to apprise her of my arrival. It being the Saturday of the sacrament, I accompanied her to Anderston, and heard sermon in the churchyard there: the crowd being so great, I lost sight of her. But after sermon, having observed me engaged in a dispute with a man from Irvine, whom she knew to be an enemy of Mr White's, she came forward, and taking my part of the argument, confuted him in all he could advance, so quickly, that I was quite surprised. As she had so many visitors from Irvine, I did not see her again till Monday, when I called at her house, and went with her to hear Mr White's trial, which was to take place that day in Mr Bell's meeting-house, before the presbytery. The meeting-house being crowded to excess, I could not get so near to the assembled ministers as to hear the words distinctly of such as spoke in Mr White's case; but, there being no opposition to it, he was suspended from his office in the ministry by the unanimous voice of the whole presbytery."

As soon as the doors of the church were closed against Mr White, several of his old congregation rallied round him, clinging at the same time to his new doctrine. The most influential and zealous of these persons, were Mr Peter Hunter, writer and town-clerk in Irvine, and John Gibson, builder there. Many individuals of both sexes followed in their wake. Mrs Buchan had informed them of the apocalypse that induced her to travel from sea to sea, for the fulfilment of that holy revelation. But though thus employed for nearly ten years, she confessed that she had been only a gazing-stock to the people, and the butt of the Devil's wrath. No person was so impressed with the belief of her divine mission, as to follow her from Banffshire; nor, after her departure from her native place, did the whimsies advanced by her disturb in the slightest degree the order of any community. In Glasgow the only convert she appears to have made was Andrew Innes, to whose narrative I again revert, in order to show the formation of the Buchanite society in all its bearings:—

"I called at the lodgings of Mrs Buchan, as she was commonly named, by appointment, the morning after Mr White's trial; the Irvine people were all gone except Mrs Gibson, and as I was about to return home, Mrs Buchan and Mrs Gibson agreed to convoy me out of town, but they walked with me all the way to Kirkintulloch before I parted with them. In a few days after my arrival at Muthill, I received a letter from Mrs Gibson, from Irvine, informing me that a number of Mr White's friends there had advised him to send for Mrs Buchan, who had arrived, and was very anxious that I should cast my lot amongst them. This I soon resolved to do, although most violently opposed by my mother and many of my friends; but my sister Margaret having assisted me privately with some small necessaries which I required, I set out for Irvine, and arrived there on the second day after leaving Muthill, and

Our Friend Mother in the Lord, as she was henceforth called, gave me a very welcome reception."

Mr White at that time preached in his own garden, but his hearers were often disturbed by evil-disposed persons throwing stones and bricks among them, which forced him to discontinue his preaching there, and his own house thenceforth became the tabernacle of the new religion. These meetings are thus described by Mr Innes :—

"When we went at night to Mr White's house, *She* (Mrs Buchan) always rose and took us by the hand, and inquired if we got in unhurt, and if so, we were desired to take a seat, and she commonly stood before us : it was all the same to her whether it was male or female, she repeated all that had passed through the day. If Mr White happened to be engaged in dispute with any of the town's-people, who were commonly the relations of some of his friends, she would point to any one that came in during that time to take a seat, and she seldom interrupted him, unless referred to in the dispute ; but if the strangers went away before we did, she commonly caused some person to stand before her, and to him she directed the whole of the points of the disputed subject, making them, as she went along, as clear as a sunbeam. At parting she shook hands with every individual, and Mr White did so also.

" The room was always crowded to excess ; and the enemies sometimes remained after the public service was over, to contend about disputed points of doctrine, from which no good resulted to either party. The friends and relations of those who had become members of the society in Irvine, were, like mine, determined to throw every possible interruption in their way. Customers had deserted merchants who had become members of the society; tradesmen, labourers, were thrown out of employment; parents were set against their children, and children against their parents, servants against their masters, and masters against their servants, and drunken sailors were encouraged to watch and molest every person about to enter Mr White's house in the evenings; and this practice not being discouraged by the magistrates, they grew the longer the more presumptuous, till at last they attacked the doors and windows with sticks and stones, and when he applied to the magistrates for protection, he was only told to send away that offensive woman, and the people would be as quiet as formerly."

For greater privacy, they subsequently met at night in the house of Mr Hunter, but their meetings there being discovered also, and the indignation of the populace being roused by the reports circulated of their doctrines and manner of worship, the doors and windows were demolished,[1] and Mrs Buchan, endeavouring to escape from the fury of the mob by a back way, was intercepted. She was accompanied by Mr Gibson, a very strong man, who, when one of the rabble was about to lay violent hands on her, grasped her round the waist with his arms, and would not part with her till a drunken fellow cut

[1] Statistical Account, by Sir John Sinclair, vol vii.

one of his hands with a jocteleg. A general shout of joy was instantly raised for the capture of the witch-wife who had "cast her glaumery" over the minister.[1] After dragging her through all the streets of the town, nearly in a state of nudity, many were for ducking her in the river, but the majority was for hounding her home to her husband, to the sound of an old tin kettle! and they actually trailed her to Stewarton, a village eight miles distant from Irvine, on the road to Glasgow. Andrew Innes says:—"Mr White and I, concealed by the darkness of the night, followed at a short distance all the way. We heard them anon insult her about her feigned attachment to Christ. They would raise her up as high as they could, calling aloud for her to fly now to heaven like Enoch or Elijah, at the same time letting her drop to the ground, exclaiming, 'She cannot fly yet, we must take her on a little further, and try her again!' When they came to a bridge at Stewarton, they took her to the ledge, for the purpose of throwing her into the river, and would have done so, had not one of the party opposed them, saying, 'She has done us no personal harm, therefore we will not kill her outright—let her husband do that if he pleases when he gets her home.' This timely interposition seemed to divert them from their intention of drowning her. As they dragged her into Stewarton, the noise which they made in the street caused the people to come running out, many with candles in their hands; the crowd soon became very great, and

[1] Appendix, Note 1.

the night being very dark, they lost sight of her suddenly, nor could they find her again.

"Mr White and I went on the Glasgow road a short way, supposing that she might have proceeded in that direction, but not finding her, and the night continuing to be very sleety, we returned home. By the way we were recognised by different straggling parties returning to Irvine, who grossly insulted us, but did not attempt to lay violent hands on us.

"We were, with Mr and Mrs Gibson and a few others, assembled in Mr White's parlour, mourning for her loss, and the opinion was gaining ground among us that she had actually ascended to heaven, when in she stepped in the grey of the morning, in a most pitiable plight: she was bare-headed, barefooted, with scarcely a rag to cover her nakedness, and all her person covered with blood; yet she was cheerful, and said, 'I suffer all this freely, for the sake of those I love.'

"On escaping from the hands of her enemies at Stewarton, she made her way back to Irvine, by climbing over dykes and squeezing through hedges, not daring to keep the public road, lest they might be in pursuit of her. All present considered the presence of a surgeon necessary, but were afraid to send for one, lest it might lead to a discovery of her return. Mrs Gibson therefore washed and dressed her wounds, and, when she was put to bed, we each retired to our respective places of abode.

"In the afternoon, when I thought she would be somewhat recovered, I went again to Mr White's house, where mostly all our friends were assembled. This was the signal for another attack. The street was soon crowded, the doors and windows were battered with stones, and attempts were made to force the doors. The magistrates convened and sent for Mr Hunter, and told him, after a great deal of discussion, that the offensive woman must be immediately removed, otherwise both lives and property would be destroyed. Seeing no other thing would do, Mr Hunter engaged a man with a horse and cart to take her to Glasgow. Mrs Gibson volunteered to attend her there, and act as sick-nurse till she recovered, and I was appointed to accompany them, for the purpose of bringing back the news of their arrival. Many of the Irvine people followed us for several miles, cursing us all the way, and threatening, that if ever she returned again, they would certainly kill her. When night came on, they returned, and we reached Glasgow, before day-break next morning, in peace."

It appears from one of Mrs Buchan's letters, that some persons in Banffshire, who took an interest in her welfare, feared that, in following out her religious pursuits, she would neglect the interests of her family; and their apprehensions appear to have been well founded. She was too much occupied with spiritual concerns, to pay any attention to household affairs. She received so many visitors in Glasgow, that her husband was reduced to abject poverty, by the extension of her hospitality to crowds of persons who were utter strangers to him. When put out of

Irvine, she was not possessed of coin even to the amount of a shilling. Andrew Innes gave her his watch, which he understood she pawned for a few shillings to supply her immediate wants, but when she received a further supply from her more wealthy adherents, she redeemed the pledge, and returned it to its proper owner.

As soon as she had somewhat recovered from the injuries she had received, she wrote to Mr Gibson:—

"Glasgow, 31st October 1783

"My dearest beloved child in the bowels of God, Son of Jesus Christ, in whom the whole family of our Lord, both in heaven and on earth, is named, in this station and relation, I have loved thee, and will love thee, world without end. With tears of joy I think of your love in the Lord for me amidst the generation of vipers, &c.

"In tribulation let us rejoice in the true way, where there is no destroyer—for the destroyers of this world are all coming against us like bulls of Bashan, with their mouths wide open, to devour all that come in their way; but my joy is to suffer—for my elder brother Jesus Christ was made perfect by suffering. . . .

"Give my love in Jesus to my dear Mr White, and to your nephew John Stephenson. I cannot forget him in faith and love. I wrote more than I intended, but I shall wrap it up in your wife's letter. This from your sister in the Lord,

"Elspath Simpson."

Friends from Irvine visited her almost daily in Glasgow, to whom she expressed the strongest desire to return again to Irvine, notwithstanding the usage she had recently received; but some of her friends were averse to her making what they regarded as a hazardous attempt, considering the state of the public feeling there against her. Having received a letter of invitation to go to Muthill, it was consequently arranged that she should go to Perthshire, and be accompanied by Andrew Innes, for the purpose of introducing her to his friends. Immediately before her departure, she wrote thus to Mrs Muir of Irvine :—

"Glasgow, November 1783.

"Oh, my dearly beloved, I cannot write with dry cheeks. The thought that I have to go further from you, is like to burst my heart; my grief is now overflowing; but it is well that I am aware of new wine having been put into new bottles. I thought to have seen you on Saturday evening, [the night of the riot, when she was put out of the town,] and to have spent the night with you in Mr White's house; but I have not the least reluctance at my sufferings there; they are now to me no more than a dream, or a tale that is told. All my joy is yet in Irvine. I do not fear any more attacks of the same kind, for I have been baptized into Christ, and I shall be like him in his resurrection. . . . .

"I would have wrote you more, but I am desirous to speak to my friends, who have come here to the communion, *as much as possible. I wish to improve every moment of my time, for you know there is no work or device in the grave, whither we are all hastening.* . . . Perhaps this letter may trouble you, but I must vent my grief. You may let Mr White see it, but it is not to be common among all my friends.—Your sister in God,

"Elspath Simpson.[1]

" P.S.—My dear, I will long more for an answer to this letter than ever I did for any, for I see that Satan is trying to *sift you;* but you have an advocate with the Father, even Jesus Christ. Look up to him, and be ye saved, for he is God, and there is nothing too hard for him to do, *only he will not go out of his way.*"

Mrs Gibson, who carried the preceding communication to Irvine, was also the bearer of the following letter to Mrs Muir's uncle, who had become one of the Friend Mother's most violent enemies :—

To Mr Hugh Allen, Irvine.

"Glasgow, Nov. 1783.

"Dearly Beloved,

"God the Father delights to show mercy to all men; yea, even to the chief of sinners. My heart feels for you, my eyes weep for you, lest you be swallowed by the devil. I was not a little surprised when I heard of your proceedings against me; yet I still covered your conduct with the most favourable construction that your actions

[1] MS. Letter-book, pp. 71, 73

would admit of; for when it was represented to me that you were really about to take my life; still I said, surely that cannot be his intention, as I was not aware of ever having done you any harm; and besides, the last time I saw you I was treated with more kindness than a cup of cold water, and that in the name of a disciple; therefore I will render thee blessing for cursing. You may call my affirming that I belong to God, blasphemy; but, seeing that such has been the accusation against the godly in all ages, I think nothing of it. I keep a record of all the good I receive from any person, but I never mind the evils—the winds carry them away like chaff.—Yours, &c. ELSPATH SIMPSON."

Mrs Innes had arrived at Irvine on the evening of the riot, whither she had gone, in the hope of persuading her son Andrew to return home. She was now happy in the thought of his doing so, even in the company of Mother Buchan. On her return to Muthill, she related all that had befallen that luckless lady in Irvine, and of her removal to Glasgow, which induced Duncan Robertson, a pious wheelwright in Muthill, to send her the letter of invitation before-mentioned, to become his guest as soon as she was able to undertake the journey. This being in accordance with the wishes of her friends in Irvine, she acquainted him with her intention of accepting his kind offer, and named the day she intended leaving Glasgow.

Relying on this intimation, Duncan sent a riding-horse to meet her at Kilsyth, and assist her on her journey; but having been detained a day longer there than she expected, she did not arrive there in time to benefit by his kindness.

Mr Innes, in his narrative, gives a detailed account of her journey from Glasgow to Muthill, but in this instance I prefer her own words :—

To the Rev. Hugh White, Irvine.

"Muthill, 16th Nov. 1783

" MY DEAREST DEAR,

"I left Glasgow on Thursday morning, on foot, with Andrew Innes, and arrived here on Friday evening. I stood it out pretty well till I had passed Stirling. I then began to be so heavy in spirits at being removed so far from Irvine, that I was like to lose all bodily strength. I said nothing of this to Andrew, but I daresay he saw it in my looks. I must remark, however, an instance of kind Providence. There came up a coach and four horses; the coachman stopped the horses after they were past us, and the coach being empty, he with great cheerfulness gave us a seat in it, and took us all the way to Muthill, where we were received in the most friendly manner. Any fruit that is appearing here, is like what was in your little vineyard at Irvine. They are thirsting for the water of life, and they receive it greedily. . . . .

"I have conversed with some of your relations, and they heard me with seeming patience; they showed the greatest fondness to see you here, and some here wish you to remove with your family to this place, to remain all winter; but at this I am silent, for I cannot think of your leaving your little society, for I love you and all your concerns. . . . . Let me vent my passion on your wife and sweet babes. O for a sight of Mr and Mrs Hunter! I would then tell them about the terrors of the night, and the arrows that fly by day, of which they are so much afraid. Give my fond love in faith to Mr and Mrs Garvin—they are my debtors both in love and letters; to James Stewart and his wife, to William Lindsay and his wife, to Elizabeth Dunlop, Thomas Niel, Keaty and John Gardner, John Bryden, Janet Carr, Johny Henderson, Jeany Watt, and my loving friend Agness Wylie, and to Mrs Young. My concern for her is, and has been, very great. O! that she may mind that time is short and eternity long. Give my love in the Lord to Mary Douglas and her brother. We have just received a letter from Mrs Gibson, which gives us great joy. *I am happy to hear that she has given a Bill of Divorcement to herself.*

"Andrew Innes's mother has her love to you, and nothing will satisfy her but having you and your family here. She says, if you cannot come here, she will go to you.—Farewell, my dearest in the Lord; all that is mine is thine.

"ELSPATH SIMPSON.

"P.S. 20*th Nov.*—My body is loaded with a great cold, but my senses are like pipes of new wine, all running from a free fountain. If the weather holds good, I trust you will make no delay in coming here *while the edge is on the people's minds.* As to removing your family, you need say little about that till you come here yourself. I am happy to hear, from Magdaline's letter to Andrew Innes, that you got safe home. Mrs Muir sent a letter to Andrew Innes, upbraiding me of drunkenness. I cannot understand what she means. She says I am a woman grieved in spirit, and cannot be comforted."

Mr Innes, in his note on this communication, says, " I was the bearer of this letter to Mr White, which he immediately obeyed. He, James Stewart, Agnes Wylie, and myself, set out from Irvine on foot in the latter end of November, and arrived at Muthill, a distance of seventy-six miles, in two days."

As soon as Mrs Buchan received an explanation of the charges complained of in her last letter to Mrs White, she wrote to Mrs Muir again in a more friendly strain than usual,—

"Muthill, November 1783

" My dear,

" You say my love for you is not so ardent as you could wish—my love to you is not flashy, nor of a fleeting nature—I cannot love to-day and hate to-morrow; indeed, I am loaded with love to the saints in Irvine, for my delight and pleasure is there, and no wonder, for they and I shall rejoice together world without end. Nothing can satisfy me till I see you all face to face, for it is Satan's plot to keep us asunder. I have received many letters from my dear friends in Irvine, but the most agreeable I ever received in the course of my pilgrimage, was from Mr James Garvin, and, on his account, I will praise, bless, magnify, and adore the fulness of a Godhead, in time and in eternity, for waiting on him, and drawing him from the depth of black nature, and landing him on new covenant ground. Give the love of Christ Jesus that is manifest in my body to him, and give him this for his comfort, *he is created again in Christ Jesus in righteousness and true holiness.*

"I am certain I afflicted you by the account I gave you of my grieved spirit, but I am no better yet, nor can I get it concealed—it is very distressing to my friends. There are not a few young creatures here that have some breathings of love, but they are like to be choked with ignorance. There is a great desire, and a great need of Mr White here. They say the ministers are shaking for fear of his coming.

"I hear that you have no view of a house and shop for the ensuing year. Leave thy lot to God, for he careth for thee, and you must learn obedience by sufferings. It seems you have been grieved for writing in such a style to Andrew Innes concerning me; but take no notice of that, for I never mind any person's disrespect for me. I have met with many acts of kindness from you, which I never will forget. —Give my love to Peggy and Annie Buchan, and to all my loving friends.

"ELSPATH SIMPSON."[1]

---

[1] MS. Letter-book, p. 71.

The comment of Mr Innes on this letter is in these words:—" Mr Garvin was deacon of the squaremen corporation of Irvine, and carried on an extensive business in his line. He had been always only a lukewarm attendant at our meetings: his conscience would not permit him to be an enemy, and the fear of losing his trade prevented his making a public declaration of his faith, but his letter had revived her hopes of his persevering. She, however, was disappointed, as he still continued in the same lukewarm state, for he never left Irvine to join the society.

" Mrs Muir was to be deprived of her shop and dwelling-house for her attention to our Friend Mother, and her friendship for Mr White and his family. Mrs Buchan's old daughter, Peggy, afterwards Mrs Saunders, had been servant to Mr White from the time Friend Mother first visited Irvine. Her youngest daughter, Anne, afterwards Mrs Goldie, had also been some time in Irvine. These are the young women whom she afterwards gave out to be—' one an incarnation of Christ, and the other of the Holy Ghost.'"[1]

Mr White accepted the invitation to Muthill, but was not so kindly received there as his female forerunner had been. "During my absence," continues Innes, " Friend Mother had visited my old aunt, to whom my sister was sick-nurse, without being molested or insulted; but the parish minister, a Mr Scott, appointed a day of visiting in the village, and

[1] Trial of the Rev. Edward Irving, edited by the Rev. Dr Duncan of Ruthwell. Dumfries edition, 1837, p. 106.

set them all in fear for the safety of the established religion, and for the Confession of Faith, which their forefathers had sealed with their blood. He strongly advised them to keep at a distance from the abominations taught by Mrs Buchan, and confirmed by Mr White.

"When Mr White did appear among them, and openly exposed, in his preaching, the errors of the Confession of Faith, many of the men who had assembled to hear him, rose to their feet, and waved their staves before him in a very threatening manner. In many respects, he resembled Stephen with the Jews, and was treated in nearly a similar manner, only he escaped unhurt.[1]

"Mr White had several old acquaintances in Muthill, but they refused to admit him into their houses, or to take him by the hand, or to touch him, as it was confidently believed he was bewitched by our Friend Mother, and they were afraid of being smitten by him if they allowed him to come near them. Mr White became discouraged, and soon left the place. Friend Mother went with him, fully as much against his consent as with it, for he was afraid of the Irvine

---

[1] "On various points of dogmatic theology he used to descant with great fierceness, and on the terrors of the law, which seemed favourite ground, as it was frequently occupied. We cannot better state the opinion entertained of him than by employing the terms in which we have heard that opinion expressed in the way of exclamation—' O ye never heard the like of it! O he was most tremendous!'' This description was given by no means in the way of objecting to his preaching the law as well as the gospel, but to the rough handling to which he subjected the word of God."—Christian Journal, vol. i., p. 306. July 1842.

people rising again. I also returned to Irvine, accompanied by several members of my family, and we shortly afterwards were followed by others, at the head of whom was Duncan Robertson, the wheelwright, who became a distinguished member of the society."

The members of the Relief congregation of Irvine who did not adhere to Mr White after his dismissal from office, entertained a hope that poverty would make him recant, and that the Buchanites would thereby be scattered; and the relations of the Irvine people who had joined the society, did all they possibly could to annoy them. But when they saw cart after cart arrive from Muthill, laden with people, goods, and chattels, their rage again became ungovernable. They assembled in the streets in crowds, and proceeding in a body to the front of Mr White's house, they pelted the windows with stones and bricks till they were all broken.

The magistrates received various petitions and applications to cause Mrs Buchan to be apprehended and proceeded against legally as a blasphemer, and Mr White, also, as a supporter and propagator of her dogmas; but they thought it more prudent to banish her from the burgh.[1] They accordingly met in council on the morning of the May fair 1784, at ten o'clock, and unanimously decreed, that Mrs Buchan should be sent forth of the royalty within two hours from that time.

---

[1] Sir John Sinclair's Statistical Account of Scotland, vol. vii, p. 183

"As the news of this decision," says Mr Innes, "soon reached all concerned, we assembled with all speed in Mr White's house, but such was the hurry, that some had scarcely time to pack up a hand-bundle, put out the fire, and lock the door. The founder of our society only was required to leave the town, but those from Muthill, in particular, were already nearly destitute for her sake, and they individually were resolved to share her fate, as were many of the Irvine people also.

"With this intention we had rallied round her in Mr White's parlour, each man with a staff in one hand, and a small bundle in the other, each woman with her coats kilted, and a small bundle in a handkerchief tied round her waist. Mr and Mrs White seemed rather downcast, but Friend Mother was more cheerful than ordinary. She spoke to us individually, and quoted passages of Scripture with surpassing aptitude, to fortify our minds in that trying hour. She often repeated the 28th verse of the 16th chapter of Matthew, with great composure and dignity. 'Verily I say unto you, there be some standing here which shall not taste of death till they see the Son of Man coming in his kingdom.' When the magistrates and constables appeared at the door, she proceeded with them, Mr White accompanying her on one side, and Mr Gibson on the other. The women and children followed, the men bringing up the rear.

"The streets through which we passed were crowded to such an excess, that the constables could scarcely open a passage. All those that came from Muthill were very ill used; the people made sport of pushing their staves between our legs so as to make us fall, and then pushed others over us, chiding us, at the same time, for ruining ourselves by following an old witch-wife who had evidently cast her cantrips over us. Just as the magistrates were about to return, a drunken sailor tore off the cap of our Friend Mother, and pulled her to the ground, and then ran past the magistrates, exclaiming. 'I have got a right handful of her hair,' and joined his companions without being interrupted or molested by the authorities."[1]

Three months after the above event, we find Robert Burns writing to a relation in Montrose an account of the sect. There cannot surely be found on record another instance of a female promulgating so publicly and obstinately the libertine principles ascribed by Burns to Dame Buchan. This letter is as follows:—

"Mossgeil, August 1784.

"MY DEAR SIR,

"We have been surprised by one of the most extraordinary phenomena in the moral world which I daresay has happened in the course of this century. We have had a party of Presbytery Relief, as they

---

[1] "In May 1784, petitions were presented to the magistrates, in which, by the Dissenters as well as Churchmen, the magistrates were called upon to apprehend her and to proceed against her as a blasphemer. They did not do this, but proceeded to dismiss her from Irvine. To protect her from insult, the magistrates accompanied her about a mile out of town; but, notwithstanding their efforts, she was grossly insulted by the mob, thrown into ditches, and otherwise ill-used by the way."—Statistical Account of Scotland: Irvine, Ayrshire. Edit. 1842

call themselves, for some time in this country. A pretty thriving society of them has been in the burgh of Irvine for some years past, till, a short time ago, a Mrs Buchan from Glasgow came among them, and began to spread some fanatical notions of religion among them, and in a short time made many converts, and among others their preacher, Mr White, who on that account has been formally deposed by his brethren. He continued, however, to preach in private to his party, and was supported, both he and their spiritual mother, as they called old Buchan, by the contributions of the rest, several of whom are in good circumstances, till in last spring the populace rose and mobbed Mrs Buchan and put her out of the town. On which all her followers voluntarily quitted the place likewise, and with such precipitation that some of them never shut the door behind them—one left a washing on the green, another a cow bellowing at the crib, without food or any body to mind her. . . . .

"Their tenets are a strange jumble of enthusiastic jargon. Among others, she pretends to give them the Holy Ghost by breathing on them, which she does with postures and practices that are scandalously indecent. They likewise dispose of all their effects, and hold a community of goods, and live nearly an idle life, carrying on a great farce of pretended devotion in barns and woods, where they lie and lodge altogether, and hold likewise a community of women, as it is another of their tenets that they can commit no moral sin. I am personally acquainted with most of them, and I can assure you the above mentioned are facts."[1]

It might be supposed that Burns merely repeated unwittingly those scandalous charges, invented by some enemy of the sect, were his statements not confirmed by their own writings.[2] In the Divine Dictionary, said to have been indited by Holy Inspiration, and published by Mr White as containing the faith and practice of the Buchanites, we find these words:—" This world has vexed themselves in vain about our views of marriage; accordingly, to all denominations we make the following information:—

" The same law that finished the carnal service at the altar, and bestial sacrifices, put an end to carnal

[1] Cunningham's Life and Works of Burns, vol. vi., pp. 46, 47.
[2] Mr Innes assures me that Burns wrote also a long poem on the Buchanites, beginning—

> " This wicked ane frae Glasgow came,
> In April eighty-three;
> And lodged her spawn among the sawn,
> An' now her fry we see."

Although I have made every search, I have only discovered a few verses of this poem; they relate merely to the ancient burgh of Irvine being the seat of presbytery for upwards of a hundred years, during which time several eminent ministers dispensed the gospel there, among whom were famous Warner and Mr Night, in whose time Hugh White would not have dared to propagate his Buchanite doctrines. David Seller, the friend of Burns, about this time employed his pen in writing the following epitaph on Luckie Buchan—

> " Stop, stranger, here lies one interred,
> Who was on earth by some revered
> And superstitiously adored,
> As the great Saviour and Lord;
> Till death, stern, cruel, unrelenting,
> In murder steeled, far past repenting,
> Sent off at ance, it mak's na' whither,
> Her Godhead and her soul thegither."

—See Poems by David Seller, printed at Kilmarnock 1789, p 234.

marriages. It is devilish to think that merely refraining from woman and certain meats, constitutes salvation. Where the Holy Spirit of God occupies all the person, and reigns throughout the flesh, it matters not much whether they marry or not.

" The people of this generation cannot be persuaded to embrace our faith and practice, and that because we are so unlike the world. Our dissimilitude to the world, must be a convincing proof that we are right. To be like the world, is to be like the devil, the father of unbelief."

The early letters of Mother Buchan are subscribed Elspath Simpson, although it was not till after her ejectment from Irvine, that she was legally divorced from her husband. In a letter addressed to the Rev. Gabriel Russell, Dundee, she writes thus :—" As for self-denial, my dear, it would not do with me to be self-denied, but even averse to self-denial." This she affirmed was all in accordance with Scripture. In the Innes MSS. we find, p. 75, that " the most legal union marriage could afford, became null and void in the society, such being at variance with the rules; it being absolutely necessary for those who had wives, to live as if they had none."

Further proofs will be added to the number of these revolting avowals; but we presume enough has been said here, to show the real cause of Mrs Buchan having received such treatment at the hands of the people of Irvine.

CHAPTER II.

The Buchanites' journey to Nithsdale—Their habitation and unrestrained manner of life there described—An armed crowd assemble at night to drive them out of that locality—Luckie Buchan and White escape the fury of the mob, but are again assailed at the Manse of Wamphray—Mrs Buchan's epistolary correspondence—Divine Dictionary—Extracts from that singular work—Blasphemous pretensions of Mother Buchan—The destruction of the world circumstantially described.

THE magistrates of Irvine did not conceive that either Mr White or any of the inhabitants of the town, who had continued to countenance his new-fangled doctrines, would actually leave their place of abode, to follow Mrs Buchan they knew not whither. " But," says Mr Innes, " there was an opinion firmly conceived among us, that some signal judgment would speedily befall the town of Irvine, such as destroyed Sodom of old, as a punishment for the usage received at the hands of the wicked people of that devoted place by our unoffending friend. Under the belief that such a manifestation of divine displeasure would soon overtake their locality, John Gibson and several of the persons accompanied us, lest, by remaining, they might suffer in the general destruction."

Mr Ayton of Hamilton, the celebrated agriculturist,

appears to have witnessed the departure of the Buchanites from Irvine. " I have been," says he, " an attentive observer of the freaks and feelings of mankind for the last seventy years, and I was not surprised to see a considerable portion of the Relief congregation of Irvine leave their homes, and set out, as they said, to heaven, under the direction of a hypocritical old woman and a wrong-headed priest, singing on the way to the New Jerusalem."[1]

Several old people still remember seeing the Buchanites on this occasion. Mrs Buchan, attired in a scarlet cloak, the discarded minister, and one or two of her higher dupes, were seated in a cart, while the remainder of the company followed on foot.[2] These were, for the most part, " clever chiels, and bonny, spanking, rosy-cheeked lasses, many of them in their teens. They were generally dressed in the simple garb of peasant maids of the Lowlands of Scotland. Over their dark petticoats, they wore short gowns, reaching from the chin half-way down the thigh, and fitted close to the bosom. They were bareheaded, and their locks, permitted to grow unusually long, were restrained from falling in a fleece over the back and bosom by small buckling-combs.[3]

" To think that so many respectable people were so completely overcome by blind fanaticism, and that such a circumstance should happen almost in the cradle of the old Covenanters, within the memory,

---

[1] Dumfries Courier, 19th June 1839. Appendix, Note 2.
[2] Contemporaries of Burns, Appendix, p. xv Edinburgh, 1840.
[3] Castle-Douglas Miscellany

too, of many persons yet alive, is the more wonderful the more one thinks of it."[1]

The progress of these enthusiastic visionaries is thus described by our native bard, Allan Cunningham. "Some were in carts, some were on horseback, and not a few were on foot. Our Lady, so they called Mrs Buchan, rode in front on a white pony, and often halted to lecture them on the loveliness of the land, and to cheer them with food from what she called the garden of mercy, and with drink from a large cup called the comforter."[2]

May 1784.—How different is the account of this journey, as recounted by Mr Innes! "When the magistrates and constables left us, a little way out of the town of Irvine, we halted on the road, and after consulting a short time as to what course we should take, we agreed to keep our faces as steadily as possible towards that part of the heavens where we supposed the Saviour of the world would appear at his second coming, agreeably to Mathew, chap. xxiv. which sayeth, 'As the lightning cometh out of the east, and shineth towards the west, so shall the coming of the Son of Man be.' We moved off very slowly along a bye-road towards the village of Mauchline, always accompanied by a crowd of spectators from the houses we passed on our journey, surprised to see so many well-dressed good-looking people travelling in such a manner. All vociferated their conviction of the truth of the common assertion, that the witch-

---

[1] Sir John Sinclair's Statistical Account of Scotland, vol. vii
[2] Cunningham's Life and Works of Burns, vol vi., p 40

wife from Glasgow had cast her cantrips over us all; and, as if afraid of being smitten in like manner by our presence, when any of us proceeded towards a house for the purpose of purchasing provisions, the people, in several instances, either fled from the house, or shut the door against us. But as we proceeded on our journey, the people, having previously heard less concerning us, were not so much alarmed. When we could get a few cakes to purchase at a farm-house, we sat down on the bank of the next stream or rivulet we came to. Our Friend Mother broke the cakes and gave each a piece, then one of the women followed with a tankard of water, and we handed it round. Thus, a piece of oat-cake, and a drink of cold water, was our common fare: we all shared alike except Friend Mother, who, after she had divided the bread, *lighted her pipe and took a smoke of tobacco.*

"Mr White was always ready to compare our situation to some circumstance in the life of Christ or his apostles, and nothing was to be seen but contentment in every face, and thankfulness in every word, that we were thought worthy of being likened to them, without having in the beginning any desire about it. Mr White also said, frequently, when we met with difficulties on our journey, that we were now suffering from the flood of the Irvine dragon's wrath, spewed out against the woman and her seed, but we had nothing to fear, for the earth would help the woman, and she would get free.

"Our number being forty-six, (this number was subsequently considerably augmented, chiefly by persons from England,) few public houses could accommodate us; and, as we were not money spenders, they were careless about our company. We had great difficulty in procuring lodgings. The first night we were permitted to occupy a cart-shed and a killogie, near Dundonald, merely because Mr Dykes, the proprietor, supposed our situation to be somewhat similar to the old Covenanters, from whom he was descended. Auchinleck was our next stage; we there obtained admission into a public-house, but only a few could be accommodated with beds. At New Cumnock we were allowed the use of a hay-loft, and were comfortable that night. At Slunkford, we solicited the use of the farmer's barn, but were refused, nor would he allow us to lay in the lee side of his hay-stack; nor were we much better situated at Edonhall. But when we arrived at Kirkconnel, on Saturday evening, we got two nights' comfortable lodgings, and the use of a large room in the public house on Sabbath, in which Mr White preached to as many of the people of the village as could gain admittance. The people heard him quietly, which was seldom the case, but they went away seemingly dissatisfied with his doctrine. At Thornhill, the people prevailed on Mr White to preach again, but as he still *used the rod of iron severely,* though they continued to hear him quietly, they were evidently much dissatisfied with the tenor of his subject.

" As we travelled on foot, our progress was retarded by Mrs White and Mrs Hunter having each two young children; but we were otherwise annoyed in the course of our journey." Besides his business as town-clerk and writer, Mr Hunter had a large concern in the shipping and coal trade of Irvine, and was known to be wealthy. Some of his friends, grieved at what they considered folly and ill behaviour on his part, in leaving his business and property, to wander with his family he knew not whither, under pretence of his having left certain parts of his extensive affairs in great confusion by his sudden departure, wherein many interests, besides his own, were involved, a fugie-warrant was obtained against him, the real object of which was to bring him back and detain him till the witch-wife was out of the way, and thereby, if possible, to break the spell under which he appeared to be labouring. A messenger-at-arms, and a troop of constables, were despatched to carry this plan into execution. They overtook the wandering Buchanites on their march, and apprehended Mr Hunter, but his wife and children were not detained, and they consequently prosecuted their journey. Several other persons from Irvine, afraid of similar consequences, returned with Mr Hunter, to settle their affairs also.

The existence of the society being thus threatened by so unexpected a deprivation of its most wealthy and zealous members, it was thought prudent by the wanderers to halt at the first resting-place they could find, there to await the return of their friends who had been separated from them. This was at New Cample, a farm in Nithsdale, two miles south of the burgh of Thornhill, thirteen miles west of Dumfries, and not more than one and a half miles from the cave where the hunted Covenanters used to conceal themselves to evade pursuit, and which Sir Walter Scott describes as having been occupied by Balfour of Burley. It is somewhat singular, that, a century afterwards, another class of enthusiasts should find a retreat in the same locality.

In journeying towards New Cample, these devotees, as if to attract general attention, made the hills and woodlands ring with hymns of their own composing, sung in full chorus, to what is called profane music. On this subject, Burns says—" When I was in Ayrshire, ' The beds of sweet roses' was a very popular song. I remember to have heard those fanatics, the Buchanites, sing some of their nonsensical rhymes, which they dignified with the name of hymns, to this air." As the attributes of the Almighty, the cardinal virtues, and even the beauties of external nature, appear to have been excluded from the Buchanite psalmody, their rhymes could not be of an elevated character, as will be shown in the course of this sketch.

The members from Irvine not returning to headquarters so soon as expected, Andrew Innes was sent back from Thornhill in quest of them, with the following letter, addressed to Janet Grant, otherwise Mrs Muir, and her servant Agnes Wylie, with both of whom the reader is already acquainted. The postscript is addressed to Mr Hunter :—

" Oh, my dear sisters, you have been at a great

loss for want of the bread of life!—the words of God spoke by the Spirit of God, which is spirit and life. O Great and precious are the mysteries of godliness that have been revealed among us since you left us! but I must warn you, my dear sisters, in the name of God your father, and his son Jesus Christ, that you come out of that place [Irvine.] And now, my dear Janet, I cheerfully acknowledge that I am bound in love to you for many great acts of kindness I have had from you, and there is none of them forgotten, but they are all recorded in heaven, and in my mind while I sojourn here on earth. But we can have no rest till you be joined with us. O that you would consider that He that will come, shall come and will not tarry! The people here, some of them say and firmly believe, that we are the children of God, and would join us cheerfully, but the devil and the world, and especially the clergy, are become so uneasy, that it appears this place will not be able to bear us much longer, so that we desire you to make all speed, and let us be joined in one, in all things; and, indeed, we would rather see you here than have ten thousand letters from you. We have thought it fit to send the bearer to speak face to face with you, and he will inform you how all things are. My well beloved and my dear sisters, and my dear friend and all his followers, join me in the same mind. So I conclude that we all firmly believe that the God of peace shall bruise Satan under our feet shortly. —Fare-you-well, on paper—your faithful friend in Christ,   ELSPATH BUCHAN.

" P.S. (*To Mr Hunter.*)—Beloved Sir,—We received your letter this morning, and was happy to hear that you and the rest of our dear friends were in health; but, dear friend, yourself would have been far more acceptable. You are at a great loss in being absent from the bread and water of life. O, what misery it is to be entangled with this bewitching world! O I charge you, in the name and by the command, that you come out from among them, and be ye separate from them, for He that will come shall come, and will long to see you face to face. Your wife and children are well, and long to see you. Our dearly beloved and most faithful shepherd has his most kind love to you, and wonders at your long absence. What if you be detaining the Lord's work? There could no destruction come on Sodom, till Lot was gone out of it."

The preceding letter bears no date of any kind, but was evidently written in May 1784.

Although Mr Davidson, the tenant of New Cample, had only made a temporary grant of an empty barn to the devotional emigrants from the west; when he found that the articles of farm produce required by them were considerable, that every thing was paid for on delivery, and that his farm-work of every description was gratuitously performed, he was induced to allow them to remain for a longer period than he had at first agreed to.

" Here," says Mr Innes, " like the disciples of Christ after Pentecost, our apostolic life commenced.

'All that believed were together, and had all things common.'[1] Our money was put into a common stock, and placed at the disposal of John Gibson, as treasurer, to purchase all that might be requisite for the use of the society. All unoccupied clothes were placed under the care of Janet Grant, formerly Mrs Muir, who had kept a cloth-shop in Irvine. She had the charge of seeing them kept clean and whole, and of giving them out when a change was wanted by any person. The other women assisted in washing, in knitting, and in mending the stockings. We had tailors who mended our clothes, and coblers who repaired our shoes—all was as common as circumstances would admit, yet none was wholly idle. We all occasionally wrought gratuitously to our neighbours, and scrupulously abjured all worldly considerations for the work thus performed.[2]

" For want of accommodation in the barn, on account of so many visitors, who often kept Friend Mother and Mr White speaking all day, we were obliged to cook our scanty fare in the farmer's kitchen—which ofttimes consisted of potatoes boiled and emptied into a basket, and set on a small table,

---

[1] Acts of the Apostles, ii , 44, 45; iv 32, 34, 35 The Labadists, too, a sect that sprung up in France in the seventeenth century, had also a community of property and wives. See Buck's Theological Dictionary; London edition, 1827

[2] " They professed only to consent to this in order that they might have opportunities of bringing over others to their views."—Chambers' Biograph Dict , vol 1. p 385 " They wrought at farm work, such as hay or harvest, but always, on such occasions, kept by themselves at meal-times, before and after which they sung hymns of their own composing.'—Reminiscences of Mrs Black of Tinwald Shaws

so that those who were pleased to withdraw from hearing the controversy in the barn, might take up one with its skin on, and either dip it in a little salt, or take a bit salt herring to it, or a drop of milk, when that was attainable. But after the first rush of visitors was abated, the barn, of course, became less crowded; we then cooked there, and got our meals more regular. All sat at the same table, and partook alike of the same food, with the exception of our Friend Mother, who either served those at table herself, or was employed in directing others to do so. When the meal was over, she always pointed to one of the men to stand up before her, to whom she directed the subject of her discourse, while we all listened; after which, a hymn being sung, we separated, and she commonly went to take a walk in the fields with Mr White.

"Having neither hay nor straw for bedding, and Mr Davidson having none to give us, we were obliged to go to the moor and gather heather for that purpose. This we bound in bundles of about six feet long, and four feet broad, thereby forming a bed for two persons. These bundles were placed in a double row on the barn-floor, leaving room scarcely for a single person to pass between them. These beds were not hard, on account of the heather being closely pressed together with the tops uppermost; but we had at first no more bed-clothes than a single blanket to each bed, and all made pillows of their body-clothes. When we had nearly completed our up-putting, Mr Hunter and several other persons arrived from Irvine, and contentedly lay down on heather beds—there being now no distinction of persons among us—those who had wives, being as if they had none. But if our Friend Mother and Mrs Gibson be excepted, the women were greatly behind the men in their compliance, for there was scarcely one, either old or young, who did not retain a partial hankering after either husband or sweetheart; but, as there was no law to be put in force, and no punishment to be apprehended, it was all matter of choice with us." (This statement plainly shows, that all the responsibilities of the marriage state were given up.)

"The only children at this time in the Society, were those of Mr White and Mr Hunter; they were taken from their mothers, and given in charge to a person with whom they had been previously unacquainted. Mr White's children, being younger than those of Mr Hunter, soon lost all recollection of their parents. But, notwithstanding the regulation, that all persons were not to pay any attention to their children, Mrs Hunter always studied to preserve the affection of hers, by giving them, privately, sweetmeats, or something to draw their attention towards her, which, when her husband observed, he was very much offended at her conduct, although he was, in general, very quiet.

"Although I have used the words Master and Mistress, in the foregoing paragraph, I have done so solely for the information of the reader, as, from the time of our arrival at Closeburn, there were no such terms used among us. Mr Hunter was called Peter, Mrs Hunter, Elizabeth Frances, Mrs White, Isabel Whitehead, and so on all the rest, with the exception of her husband, who wished to be called Friend White. The author of our society was, even in Irvine, called by us, Friend Mother in the Lord, as we supposed our relation to her resembled that of Paul to Timothy—she being authoress of our religious opinions, as Paul was of those entertained by Timothy." Such is the reason now given for their living in common, by Andrew Innes. But the general belief was, and still continues to be, that it was for the purpose of committing and concealing crimes of a flagitious character.

Mr Davidson, having intimated that he would require the use of his barn as soon as his growing crop could be gathered in, and having accompanied this intimation with a proposal, that, if they would build a house for themselves, he would give them ground whereon to erect it, the offer was gladly accepted; and there being in the society suitable artisans, a house was erected before harvest time. It is thus described by Mr Innes,—" The house was only one storey high, and covered with heather—it was thirty-six feet in length, and sixteen feet wide. There was a loft in it, made of poles from a neighbouring plantation, and these were covered with green turf, instead of boards. Something like a bedstead was formed by four boards being nailed together at each end; these were laid flat on the loft, and filled with straw, as soon as we could procure it.

We had now two blankets for each bed—one below, and the other as a coverlet. The beds, now more numerous than when in the barn, were required to be placed so close together, that a person could hardly move between them. To the bed-room we ascended by a trap-ladder in the middle of the house. There were only two beds below, in a small closet adjoining the kitchen. Our furniture consisted of two long tables, or deals, surrounded by binks or cutty-stools. In the kitchen was a dresser, a meal-chest, and a few stools. In Mr White's closet was a table and a few chairs, intended for strangers."

This is an exact description of the cabin, (called by the country people, in derision, "Buchan Ha'"—a name it retains to this day,) in which were immured about sixty persons, who embraced some of the worst dogmas of the ancient Essenes, and of the modern Socialists.

Such an occurrence as the arrival of the Buchanites, could not fail to produce a strong sensation throughout Nithsdale, particularly as rumour had flown before, and prepared the way—painting their persons and principles in colours brightened or darkened according to the fancy or faith of the teller. As mentioned by Mr Innes, people flocked from a considerable distance to see Dame Buchan and her followers, whom Mr White, when addressing his hearers, and, subsequently, in his *Divine Dictionary*, described as " the mysterious woman predicted in the Revelation, in whom the light of God was restored to the world, where it had not been since the ascension of Christ, but where it would now continue till the period of translation into the clouds, to meet the Lord at his second coming."

Mr White at first preached almost daily to large assemblies of people, and the service was generally concluded with an exhortation or explanation of a more familiar nature by Mrs Buchan. But the number of hearers rapidly decreased. Mr Innes proceeds,—" Among the strangers who attended, were nearly all the neighbouring clergy, who, instead of representing what they knew to be true to others, acted like the Jews of old, who, when they could not deny the miracles of Jesus, said that he did them by the aid of Beelzebub, the prince of devils. In like manner did they affirm that she acted by the power of witchcraft—in blinding those who placed any dependance in her divine mission; thereby keeping up the people's wrath against her, and against those who were with her. When they went to their pulpits, they represented all they had heard in the worst possible light, which so inflamed the minds of the people, that, like those in Irvine, they resolved to expel us from the country.

" 24th *December* 1784.—They appointed a night for the purpose, when there was no moonlight, and the ground was covered with snow. In the evening, lights appeared on all the surrounding hills, as a signal to collect and attack. Signal guns were also fired; and, in a little time, we observed clusters of men gathering and approaching in every direction towards our house, to the number of one hundred at least, armed with bludgeons, pitchforks, and flails. When they came near, we all went in and made the door and windows as fast as possible. After surrounding the house, one person rapped smartly at the door and demanded admittance; but, on no answer being returned, the rap was repeated with greater violence, accompanied by a threat, that 'if Luckie Buchan,' using their own words, ' and the Man Child White, were not instantly turned out of the house, they would burn it and all its inmates to ashes,' at the same time making preparations to break the door; but, after a vain attempt to do so, or to wrench off the window-shutters, stones were battered against both doors and windows, till the whole was smashed in pieces. They then rushed in, but were seemingly surprised to see us all sitting as composedly as if nothing had happened.

"They then began to inspect our faces, to see if our Friend Mother was among us; but, not finding her, they enquired where she was. On being informed she was where they could not possibly find her, they became infuriated, saying they would have her if she were above ground. The beds and chests were all strictly examined, also the farmer's house and offices, and, lastly, the draw-well, but all to no purpose.

"Not finding her, they returned to us, ordering every one to turn out; and, on being instantly obeyed, they began by seizing us, one by one, by the arms, one at each side, and one pushing behind, till they got us all out of the house. They then dragged us, in every direction, through the snow, (at that time about a foot deep,) but mostly towards the Thornhill road, for the purpose of driving us home; but when they were tired of doing so, they dispersed, and we returned to our house, which was nearly in ruins. The doors and windows were all demolished, and what little furniture we had was all broken, yet the minister of the parish, notwithstanding this outrage, calls the inhabitants of Closeburn a quiet, sober, and industrious people.[1]

"We would not have been aware of this outrageous assault, till it had actually commenced, had it not been for the kindness of Mr Stewart, factor to Mr Monteith of Closeburn, who, on the preceding evening apprised us of what was to take place, and invited Friend Mother and Mr White to Closeburn Castle, till the assault was over; which invitation they reluctantly accepted, and thereby escaped the fury of the mob. Our Friend Mother would undoubtedly have fallen a victim to the fury of the rioters, had they found her. Even the people, when we worked to them gratis, never ceased accusing us of our folly in attending to her; and several of them told us that we would be worried and torn to pieces by bull-dogs, which they had procured for the purpose.

"None of the persons who dragged Mrs Buchan through the streets of Irvine, or those who broke the doors or windows and furniture of the unoffending

---

[1] Sir John Sinclair's Statistical Account of Scotland, vol xiii, p 247.

people who sheltered her from the outrageous mob, were called, by the constituted authorities, to account for their conduct in disturbing the peace of the burgh. But the rioters at New Cample did not escape the fangs of justice so easily. Upwards of twenty of these were fined at Dumfries by the sheriff of the county."[1] Mrs Buchan thus writes concerning this occurrence :—" We are daily suffering from this wicked world, so that we would not be suffered to live and walk on the earth, if the power and wisdom of God was not wonderfully displayed in laying restrictive bounds to their wrath."[2]

According to the MS. so frequently quoted, Mr White spent much of his time while at Closeburn in writing hymns, which were sung with great devotion in the society. "The people of Closeburn," nearly the first in the MS. collection, is a poor production for a man of letters. I insert a stanza of it here, merely to show the simplicity of the people who could take an interest in such a rhapsody. It consists of eight stanzas :—

"The people in Closeburn parish residing,
Came often our sermons to hear;

[1] Encyclopædia Perthensis.
[2] Letter to the Rev. Thomas Okeley, Northampton — "The sheriff interfered for their protection, and had forty-two of the rioters tried before him for the assault. The Buchanites would not prosecute. The prosecution had to be laid in the farmer's name, for injury done to his property; and even so peaceful were the Buchanites, that they would scarcely bear witness in evidence to the injury they had sustained. The first of them called as a witness had to be committed to prison for prevaricating and repressing the truth."— Scots Magazine, 1785, p. 118.

> And rudely they question'd our words, though most pure—
> Our persons they threaten'd to tear.
> They often with batons and cudgels combined,
> With billets of wood and with stones—
> But He who has power all men to control,
> Prevented them breaking our bones."

It may be recollected that some of the members of the Relief congregation of Irvine wished to hand Mrs Buchan and Mr White over to the civil authorities as blasphemers, but that the magistrates declined to act in the case. Immediately after the riot at Closeburn, they lodged a similar charge in the ecclesiastical court in Dumfries-shire, as appears from the following extract from the records of the presbytery of Penpont, obligingly made, at my request, by Mr George Hunter, clerk to the presbytery:—

" *2d February* 1785.—The presbytery, by reference from the sessions of Closeburn, the minutes bearing that Alexander Gibson and others, had libelled Hugh White and Mrs Elspath Buchan for teaching blasphemous doctrine. The presbytery sustain the reference, and resolve to proceed to the probation of the libel. They then cited said parties to appear before them; but, in apprehension of personal danger, they did not obtemper the citation, and the libellers having failed to prosecute their libel, the presbytery being fully persuaded that little progress is likely to be made by measures so conducted, found themselves under the necessity of considering the libel as deserted, and, accordingly, dismissed the said libel."

While this case was depending in the ecclesiastical court, another charge was preferred against the same parties in a district-court of the county magistrates. Mr Innes had prevailed on his brothers and sisters, six in number, to join the society, and his mother also; but the latter, being dissatisfied with their proceedings, remained only a few months at New Cample, and afterwards used every possible means in her power to cause her children, who were all grown up to the estate of men and women, to follow her example, and to return home to their former employments. Having succeeded in two or three instances, and wishing to reclaim the remainder of her strayed flock, she decoyed another son and daughter to Muthill, in the expectation of receiving a large sum of money, which she pretended had been bequeathed them by a relation recently deceased. As the funds of the society were in a declining state, Friend Mother readily consented to the legatees going to Muthill for their money; but, to ensure their return, Gibson, the treasurer, was to accompany them. "On arriving at our mother's house, they were received with an appearance of friendship; but, in a short time, a number of men entered the house, each with a large stick in his hand, to drive away Gibson, and detain Joseph and Margaret by force. The former instantly decamped, and Joseph rose to follow him; but they kept him prisoner till next day, when he forced his way, and returned to New Cample, without a single coin in his pocket, after having travelled a hundred and twenty miles. In a few days, he was followed by two constables, who demanded money for all the articles my mother had brought to Irvine, which, being refused, they obtained a warrant to take our Friend Mother and Mr White before a court of justices of the peace in the neighbourhood; but Mr White was too good a lawyer to be so easily caught. He informed the magistrates, that my mother brought all the property, for which remuneration was now claimed, of her own free will and accord; and, for any thing he knew to the contrary, she might yet find them, as she left them in Irvine; upon which the case was dismissed."

Mrs Buchan had a son in the society, who, by virtue of a warrant granted at the instance of his father, was apprehended also, and carried back to Glasgow. At the commencement of the French war, this young man entered into the naval service, and was killed at the battle of Trafalgar.

The first person who evinced an inclination to join the knot of enthusiasts at New Cample, was George Hill, a well-educated young man, who had been for some time clerk to the Closeburn Lime Works. He lived at Closeburn Castle, with Mr Stewart, on the estate of Mr Monteith, and often visited the society. Mr Hill was a native of Edinburgh; and when his relations there became aware of his being about to relinquish his situation for the purpose of becoming a Buchanite, two of his brothers proceeded to Closeburn to persuade him against taking a step calculated to ruin himself, and to bring disgrace on his family. If he had any intention of listening to the friendly advice of his relations, the following letter, opportunely delivered, fixed his resolution of becoming a Buchanite, and he accordingly joined the society:—

To Mr George Hill, Closeburn Castle.

"New Cample, 8th June 1785.

"MY VERY DEAREST DEAR FRIEND IN THE MOST ENDEARING LOVE OF GOD,—The fountain of mercy is ever full, and its stream runs free: they who drink like you have nothing to pay, for it is your Father's good pleasure to give you the kingdom of righteousness; but, my dear, you know all the streams of this fountain must be joined at the fountain-head, or else the streams would run dry.[1] You are dear to all in heaven, and also to us all, who are your fellow-travellers to that country through this land of enemies. . . . .

Give my love to Mrs Stewart. I hope she will be eternally happy. We thought to have had the pleasure of seeing Mr Stewart here before this time. You may tell him that I long to see him. *Although he should not love my way of life, nor believe in the power of God to keep me alive till his second coming, as a wonder of his free love and mercy,* he cannot hinder me to live breathing out the free love of God's blessed mercy. My love to him is, that he may be blessed among those in the New Jerusalem; and why

---

[1] These words remind me much of the following passage in Rutherfurd's Letters.—" To drink of the well of life up at the well's head is more sweet and fresh by far than that which we get in borrowed old running-out vessels, and our wooden dishes here "—Part I., Epistle 22.

should he reject it, when it is God's will to give it to him freely?—Yours in the Lord,

"ELSPATH SIMPSON."

It appears that the minister of Wamphray, a parish in Annandale, was one of the clergymen with whom "our Friend Mother" was acquainted when in Banffshire; and, wishing to renew her intimacy, she thus addresses that gentleman, and afterwards his lady:—

To the Rev. Mr Nicholson, Manse of Wamphray.

"New Cample, 11th July 1785

"MY DEAR SIR,

"Your acquaintance and mine was begun, and carried on, in the love of God. You are the first man in the world that witnessed with eyes and ears, the overflowing fountain of mercy proceed from my mouth. I have longed very much to see you and to converse with you; and had I as much freedom to walk in the land of the enemies of Jesus Christ as you have, I would have seen you long before this time. The days have been, when you would have come a further distance to see me; but you did it not without persecution even at that time.

"The world is lying in darkness and delusion; but Antichrist began to busk himself even in the days of the apostles. He, however, got little rest in his filthy rags while the true light was in the world. The light of God was given them without money and without price; but the devil and the world liked no such market. In the present day, they have the like thoughts of the Spirit of God, termed, in Scripture, the Holy Ghost, or Spirit of God on earth. . . . . Yours in the Lord,

"ELSPATH SIMPSON."

To Mrs Nicholson, Wamphray Manse.

"New Cample, 11th July 1785.

"MY VERY DEAR DEAR ANNIE,

"I have longed much to see and converse with you; but perhaps you would not wish to see me now, as my life and conversation is the very butt of the devil's wrath; even the sight of my person is an object of derision to the world; but at this I have no grudge, for I want no friendship with the world: it has mistaken *the sent of God.* I have been a wonder to the world, but I have wondered as much as they, for I have always found the people of this world like raging lions and roaring bears, foaming out their own shame. I hope you will write me a few lines by the bearer, and believe me ever, dear Annie, &c. ELSPATH SIMPSON."

These letters were followed by an invitation by Mr and Mrs Nicholson to visit them at the manse of Wamphray, which she did, accompanied by Mr White. Mr Nicholson being afraid that the visit of Mrs Buchan and her high priest, might be construed into a countenancing of the Buchanite heresy on his part, sent for two of his elders to be present during the interview. After their arrival, a religious controversy soon commenced, in the course of which Luckie boldly maintained that she was actually the Spirit of God, which all unbelievers would soon know to their cost; upon which Mr Nicholson rose from his chair, and giving her a hard clap on one of her shoulders, said—" I am sure there are both flesh and blood there, which is proof positive that you are not a spirit, as you say you are." The elders, not wishing to hear her utter such blasphemy, left the room abruptly, and in a short time a crowd assembled round the manse, and threatened to *mob* the visitants if they did not instantly depart; which, for their own safety, they were obliged to do. Mr Nicholson was speedily called in question for defiling his manse with such unholy visitors; many of his congregation became dissatisfied with particular points of his doctrine, although in no ways different from what he had formerly maintained. These circumstances tended to render him very unpopular in his parish. It was also rumoured, that he was friendly to some of the dogmas of Mrs Buchan, although he was never known to hold any intercourse with her or her coadjutor, beyond the instance just stated.

As the Buchanite heresy became more generally known, they had the more opposition to contend with at a distance. Mrs Buchan thus complains of the expense of postage—" We thank you for paying your letter, for we are much imposed on by people sending letters to us, of no use but to vex us and give us trouble." The letters written by her at this time, were numerous. They were usually all on religious subjects, expressed in the style with which the reader is already acquainted. From her correspondence I only make such extracts, as appear to me to illustrate either her character or the history of the society.

To the Rev. Gabriel Russell, Dundee.

"New Cample, —— 1785

. . . . . "O my dear, it would not do with me to be self-denied, or even denied to self-denial. I have never felt a desire of revenge against the greatest of my enemies, not even against those who have shed my blood, torn my flesh, and pulled out my hair, and threatened me with the worst of deaths; for I know they did it ignorantly through unbelief; for, my friend, this generation cannot bear to hear sound doctrine, for they have heaped up to themselves teachers, having itchings ears; they are all minding their own things, but few the things of Jesus Christ. I have been, these ten years past, the very butt of the great red dragon's wrath, and a gazing-stock to a restless blinded world, who are continually spewing out great floods of falsehood, cruel mockings, and murdering plots against us, either to scatter or kill us; but oh, praise! praise! eternal praise and thanksgiving to divine wisdom and almighty power, that the worst of their intentions have hitherto turned out for our good, for none of our society has yet fallen before the enemy! We did not leave Irvine till we were obliged to flee for our lives. We have never lacked any thing yet; it is even better with us than it was at the beginning. —Yours, &c.   ELSPATH SIMPSON."

Mr White carried on for some time a correspondence with Mr James Purvice, a schoolmaster in the neighbourhood of Edinburgh, on religious topics; but when Mr Purvice announced his intention to publish the whole correspondence, with his own remarks on the points at issue, Luckie took up the pen to express her sentiments.[1]

To Mr James Purvice, Schoolmaster.
" SIR,

"You have troubled us much with your letters, but, indeed, I was jealous of your satanic self-righteous designs. You said, in your first letter, you had heard we believed in the Millennium, and that you thought this doctrine had no small countenance from the Scripture. I think, of all the letters I have ever seen, yours are the most confused mixture of Christ and the devil. It appears to me, that you are a man who desires to show your abilities to the world. You want a proof, as the Jews of old did of Jesus, whether he was Christ or not. I answer, you had better come and see what we are, before you publish your controversy—living words have always more weight than dead letters. Not that we are afraid of

---

[1] See "Eight Letters between the people called Buchanites, and a Teacher, near Edinburgh." Edin. 1785.

you; for we are not our own—we are Christ's, and the world knoweth us not. I think I never had such a shock, as to hear, from your letter, that you marked God debtor to carnal man for bringing in children after the flesh, that he might get seed to Jesus Christ, after the flesh. . . . .

"ELSPATH SIMPSON."[1]

"When I went into Edinburgh," writes Andrew Innes, "with the second part of Mr White's work, to get it printed, Mr Purvice called on me at Mr Hill's father's house, where I lodged, and disputed with me strongly against the personality of God He said God was light, and light could not admit of personal parts; but when I directed his attention to Moses at Mount Sinai, he was put to a stand. I never saw his publication, but I believe it was published in 1786."

From the strain of Mrs Buchan's letter to Mr Purvice, and other circumstances, the announced publication seems to have caused a great sensation

---

[1] According to Mr Innes, Purvice was schoolmaster at Broughton, but the following letter from my friend Mr Paul, minister of that parish, shows that to be a mistake.

"Broughton Manse, 8th Nov. 1838

"MY DEAR SIR,

"It gladdens my heart to see your fist once more I am sorry to say, that there never was a James Purvice schoolmaster in Broughton. Mr Andrew Innes must be mistaken as to the name of the parish. If I could find any circumstance as to the name of the parish, or regarding the author of the pamphlet, so as to afford a clue, I would most willingly lend my aid to trace out particulars, for it is probable the author is not now in the land of the living.—Yours sincerely,

"HAMILTON PAUL."

amongst the little knot at New Cample.[1] The general feeling was, that, having, as they thought, Scripture to support all their dogmas, they should publish to the world such an exposition of their "Faith and Practice," as would tend, in future, to silence their enemies. The execution of this work devolved upon Mr White, who was zealously assisted by Mr Hunter, and found an active amanuensis in Mr George Hill, the young man who had recently joined the society. The first part of the work is dated 18th October 1785, and the second and concluding part, on 9th December of the same year. It comprises, in all, 124 octavo pages.

The first portion of the work was printed by Mr Jackson, in Dumfries; but he had thereby incurred such public odium, that he could not be prevailed on to publish the remainder. Mr Innes was therefore dispatched to Edinburgh on foot, with the MSS. in his pocket, but he could not find a person disposed to publish the work, till he engaged to become the purchaser of a considerable part of the impression. There being no demand for these copies, they were ultimately given away gratuitously by Mr White in Dumfries-shire and Galloway.

An idea may be formed of the strain of the work, from the copious contents of the title-page. "The

---

[1] Mr Struthers says, "Their ambition to be known in the world, made them very desirous to answer all inquiries that were put to them; and, to spread their fame, they began vauntingly to publish their correspondence." Struthers' Hist. of the Relief Church, p. 339 Christian Journal for January 1835, p. 12

Divine Dictionary, or a Treatise indited by Holy Inspiration, containing the Faith and Practice of the people (by the world) called Buchanites, who are actually waiting for the second coming of our Lord, and who believe that they alone shall be translated into the clouds, to meet the Lord in the air, and so shall be ever with the Lord. 'There appeared a great wonder in heaven—a woman.' Rev. chap. xii. v. 1. Written by that society."

The work, throughout, is a complete jumble of fanatical jargon, and denunciations against those who dared to disbelieve the divine mission of the mysterious woman; and a crude exposition of their heterodoxy, arranged under the following heads:— "Concerning the propagation of the human race—a demonstration that the soul and person is the same —the person of Christ possessed of a divine nature only—concerning the Spirit of God—concerning God's decrees—the nature of true devotion—God's method of calling men to true salvation—concerning the end of the world—a divine receipt, instructing how all may live for ever—the meeting Christ in the clouds," &c.[1]

It is mentioned in this work that, "in nothing are

[1] Their worst enemies could not have advised them to do any thing more injurious to their reputation and success, than to write a book It showed them to be illiterate, erroneous, visionary, and rhapsodical So little reason was mixed up with their madness, that it is often impossible to comprehend their ravings; and to say exactly what, on various topics, was their belief. Their favourite passage of Scripture was Heb ix 28—"Unto them that look for him shall he appear the second time, without sin unto salvation."—Struthers' History of the Relief Church

the people of the world more deluded, than in their views regarding the generation of children. They think that God puts a soul into every child that comes into the world. This leads me to think, that the world knows no more of their souls, than the beasts of the fields know of theirs. The description that this world sometimes gives of their soul, is the same as a description of nothing. The notion of a soul existing in a separate state from that of the body, is the height of absurdity;—it is the folly of heathen philosophy, which has mingled with what man calls divinity. Through the whole of the Old Testament, without an exception, the term soul denotes the whole person. The breath that went into the nostrils of Adam, was 'the life of his soul,' and the final exit of that breath was 'the death of his soul."[1]

"Men think that people are to come to the knowledge of God, some other way than by their senses; but it is nonsense, and the height of absurdity, to think that the knowledge of God and his ways, can be attained in any other way than by external organs of sense. They are only visionaries who speak of internal evidence."[2]

"I once thought, as the world now thinks, that the Spirit of God wrote the Scriptures so mystical and obscure, that there was need for what they call learned men, to explain the meaning to what is called the vulgar or less learned. I was made to believe

---

[1] Divine Dictionary, pp 14, 15   [2] Ibid p 23

that a number of years in a Grammar School, in a University, and Divinity Hall, would at least make me understand more of the ways of God, than if I had not these acquirements. But were there ambiguity in the Scriptures, would the University and Divinity Hall qualifications remove that ambiguity? Human acquirements always, without exception, make men proud or devil-like—bad qualifications to make men understand the ways of God. The person who thinks that any man can tell the mind of God more plain than God has actually done, must travel in darkness, die in darkness, and rise to inherit darkness. Flesh and blood shall neither inherit heaven nor hell; both saints, who sit in judgment, and the wicked who are judged, have bodies devoid of such feeble materials."[1]

"A great part of this world's devotion, is in their praying God to save them. What, then, must be their views of God who think that he requires pleading to be willing to save them?—salvation was never gained in this way. I tried this way of beseeching God to grant me mercy; but, although I had continued this practice a thousand years, it neither would have offended the devil, nor have benefited my own person. We must be pleased with God and his ways. Such as are pleased with him, are entered into salvation."[2]

"The world mock us, because our immortality lies in God; whereas they think there is something

[1] Divine Dictionary, pp 27, 28   [2] Ibid. pp. 33, 34

within the compass of their own bodies, unperishing in its nature. They make merry concerning our translation through the air to meet our Lord, yet every one of them thinks they have something at death, that is to be translated through the air to meet the same Jesus. They would not give the same privilege to our real souls, which they take to their imaginary ones. To hear of our translation is a matter of much astonishment to them, because we believe in a visible something to be translated. They believe that for every death happening among them, there is a translation of an unperceived nothing, extracted from some or every part of the body; but they cannot tell from what part of the body this imaginary soul takes its departure."[1]

"The mysterious woman predicted in Rev. xii., has actually appeared, and in her the light of God is restored back to this earth, and will continue here till the period of translation into the clouds to meet the Lord at his second coming. To do justice to this poor deluded world, let me tell them there is but one such light, one such individual upon the earth, or has been since the death of the holy martyr mentioned in Revelation ii. 7."[2]

"These few lines are not sent into this poor deluded world with a view to save them, but to assure them that the Spirit of God is now on earth; and that they cannot use God's time well in any other way or exercise, except by coming to this

---

[1] Divine Dictionary, p. 55   [2] Ibid.

place, [New Cample] where the light of God is, to save such as are to be saved from sin and death. . . . Let none now despise the truths contained in this publication. Never mind the style; but attend to the sentiments."[1]

The work concludes thus:—" The truths contained in this publication, the writer received from the Spirit of God, in that woman predicted in Rev. xii. 1., though they are not written in the same divine simplicity. By a babe in the love of God.

(Signed) " HUGH WHITE.

" Revised and approved by ELSPATH SIMPSON.

" New Cample, near Thornhill, Dumfries-shire,
" 9th December 1785."

In my humble opinion, Mr White shows, by his own example, that knowledge and ignorance, reason and superstition, are often divided by a thin partition; and that they not only sometimes dwell together in the same person, but also, by an unnatural and unaccountable union, lend each other mutual assistance, and thus engender monstrous productions, such as the *Divine Dictionary*. The clergy of Nithsdale might have been irritated by the distorted views of Scripture advanced in that publication, but beyond that district it was little known; the work appears to have fallen dead from the press, which is perhaps the true cause of no clergyman having lifted his pen against the heterodoxy of that declamatory work. Religious sectaries being always supported

[1] Introduction to Divine Dictionary, pp. 3, 4.

by contention, the silence of the clergy was a more deadly blow to the pretensions of the Buchanites, than all that could have been written against them.

"Mr White's plan," says Mr Innes, "for redeeming the earth from the bondage of corruption, was similar in many respects to that prescribed by St John in the Revelation. It was—'That we who were waiting with our Friend Mother at the second coming of Christ, would be personally raised, by supernatural power, like Elijah or Jesus, till we were above the ethereal heavens, where we would have a resting-place with the angels and all redeemed saints; and, in the presence of Father and Son, to be spectators of the consuming by fire of all polluted objects, under the direction of the destroying angels appointed for that purpose; there to remain until this world was consumed, and the stream of vapour rising from it while in the act of consumption, had cooled and become solid, then to remove to that new world, where Christ is to reign with the saints for a thousand years. Whilst all the pollutions created by evil men, fell down into a solid body, and formed the residence of satan, and all the offspring of his evil and polluting spirit, which, in Scripture, is called hell.'"

CHAPTER III.

The Buchanites imposed on by a dissolute officer of the Royal Marines—Andrew Innes, when on a mission into England, suddenly called home, with his converts, to meet the Lord in the clouds—The midnight manifestation at New Cample—The great Fast of forty days commenced—Several of those engaged in that wild project nearly starved to death—The fasting scheme interrupted by the interference of the county magistrates—The Buchanites suspected of the crime of infanticide—Andrew Innes dismissed from the Society—His vision at Leadhills—Mother Buchan attempts again to scale the sky—Circumstances connected with that ridiculous affair.

STRANGERS who called at Buchan Ha', either to see the internal arrangements, or to converse with the great Luminary herself, were very kindly received. One of the most noted of their casual visitors, was James Brown, a merchant tailor from Sunderland, who, being captivated with what he had seen and heard at New Cample, on his return to England, published an account of those expectants of immortality; and, on announcing his intention of becoming one of their number, was followed by several other persons, one of whom is thus spoken of in the Divine Dictionary.[1] "Upon hearing of our waiting on Christ's second coming, that we might have a victory over death, Charles Edward Conyers, a young gentleman of His Majesty's naval officers,

[1] Divine Dictionary, p. 83.

left all the vain glory of his former life, and immediately came to wait with us for the coming of Jesus."

As, up to that period, it had been a fundamental rule of the society, that no member could retain any earthly drag or entanglement, whereby his ascension could be retarded at the great day, so ardently expected to be quite at hand,[1] Mr Conyers was, consequently, required to resign his half-pay as an officer of marines, in this formal manner:—

Copy of a letter from Charles Edward Conyers, late First Lieutenant of Marines, to Philip Stephens, Esq., Secretary of the Admiralty.

"New Cample, near Thornhill, Dumfries-shire,
'5th June 1786.

"SIR,

"Be so good as inform my Lords Commissioners of the Admiralty, for His Majesty's information, that I freely resign my commission under His Majesty, being determined to hold no commission under an earthly crown. My reasons for so doing, are the

---

[1] Reminiscences of Mrs Black, Tinwald Shaws, Dumfries-shire, communicated by Mr Laurie, 15th June 1841. A gentleman from Glasgow also visited them, who gives the following account of them, (see Scots Magazine for November 1784)—" The Buchanites pay great attention to the Bible, having it always at hand They spend a great deal of their time in singing hymns, in which peculiar tenets are constantly brought forward, and in conversing about religion. They believe that the last day is at hand—that none of their number shall die; but soon shall hear the sound of the last trumpet, when all the wicked shall be struck dead, and remain so for a thousand years, while they shall live and reign with Christ on the earth."—Christian Journal for January 1835, p 12.

following :—Making a tour through the north of England, at Sunderland I met a person who informed me, that he had seen in Scotland a person imbued with the Spirit of God, with whom there were a number waiting for the return of Jesus. all believing they were among the number who should not die, but be carried into the clouds, to meet the Lord in the air. Accordingly, I proceeded to Scotland, where I have found this person illuminated by divine light.

"With these blessed expectants of immortality, I now await till clear shall shine the perfect day. From this, you will see that I am entered into a noble warfare, for a noble prize.—Yours, &c."[1]

There was not, seemingly, a more zealous member than Conyers in the society. He assisted Mr Hunter in transcribing the hymns and poems written by Mr White, into books for the use of the society. But it soon became evident that he had other motives for cooping himself from all intercourse with the world, than the hope of immediate translation to heaven, as, in the spring of the year 1786, he was apprehended at New Cample, on a charge of having defrauded a life-assurance company in London to a large amount.

The letter resigning his half-pay, which he took to Thornhill, the nearest post-town to New Cample, as he said, to put into the post-office with his own hand, in order that he might be satisfied of its

[1] Divine Dictionary, p. 111.

being really dispatched to its proper destination, was found among some other papers which he left, on being hurried away from New Cample by the officers of justice. They were afterwards satisfied that he was only a wolf in sheep's clothing, of which, had they attended to it, they had sufficient proof on his arrival. On his way from England to New Cample, he lodged for a night at Brownhill, a noted wayside inn in the immediate neighbourhood of the latter place, but, having no money to pay his way, the landlord kept his hat. His first appearance, therefore, before the mysterious lady, was bareheaded. This she looked upon as a mark of profound respect, showing a sense of the superior breeding of the young man, to which she was not always accustomed. But, on learning afterwards the true cause of Conyers' obeisance, his old hat was redeemed, although a new one might have been purchased for less money. The last appearance of this young man, without a hat, was on the scaffold at Tyburn.

Other moneyless rakes afterwards applied for admission, but not with the same success. Finding she had been deceived by Conyers, Mrs Buchan instituted an investigation and examination of suspected applicants, in which she was herself the chief actor; but with the particulars of which we cannot pollute our pages.

The next person, attracted by the representation of the Sunderland clothier to visit the Buchanites, from England, was Thomas Bradley, from Stranton, near Hartlepool, in the county of Durham; who, after remaining a few weeks with them at New Cample, returned to England to dispose of his property in Yorkshire, as well as his farming stock at Stranton. At Mr Bradley's request, Andrew Innes and Duncan Robertson, two of the chief apostles, accompanied him as missionaries, in the hope of making a few more converts in that quarter.

It may be remembered, that, after the wonderful woman seen in heaven brought forth a man child, she was to remain one thousand two hundred and threescore days in the wilderness. To fulfil the typical representation of Mrs Buchan's divine mission, her abode in the wilderness was supposed to have commenced when she converted Mr White on her first visit to Irvine — he being the man child who was to rule all nations with a rod of iron. As her fancied abode in the wilderness therefore drew near a close, the enthusiasm of her followers rose, in the hope that, at the end of that time, they would be raised with her to heaven. The following hymn, giving Mrs Buchan the antonomasia of Mercy, was composed by Mr White at that time, and was one of those usually sung to the tune of the "Beds of sweet roses."

" When Mercy's on earth, with Mercy close wait,
　Lest you be found wanting when she takes the gait
　With Mercy still tarry, with Mercy ascend;
　For saved shall be who endures to the end
　When Mercy doth call you, then hasten your pace,
　And spare not beginning a heavenly race
　When Mercy is ardent to glory to soar,
　Then tread in that path where Mercy's before

> When Mercy is weary with changes of men,
> 'Tis dreadful for you to seek rest with them then
> The ways and the courses which Mercy ne'er treads,
> Forsake, or you're sure to be found with the dead,
> When Mercy will show you, that sudden must be
> The time of departure her glory to see.
> Then wait still at home, or perhaps you may find,
> When Mercy ascends you will be left behind." [1]

So confident were they that the second coming of Jesus Christ was at hand, that Mr White wrote as follows:—

To Thomas Bradley, Stranton, near Hartlepool, county of Durham.

"New Cample, 24th April 1786

"DEAR LOVING BROTHERS AND SISTERS IN GOD,— We received your most heavenly letter on the 23d, and we rejoice to see you safe amidst so many rapacious lions seeking to devour the seed of God. Let me put you in remembrance, that you are as nearly related to the Spirit of God on earth, as the branches are to the tree on which they grow; or you are as nearly allied to God on earth, as Christ on earth was to his Father in heaven. The saints in glory are your loving brothers, and are now longing for the time of the bride's translation. Apostles, and their seed, sleeping in death, are also beginning to feel the quickening breath of God. All these circumstances cry—'Make haste! though now in the flesh, you shall soon be in spiritual bodies! You

[1] The Buchanite MS Hymn-book, p 136

now dwell with a God in grace, but you shall soon dwell with a God in glory! The Spirit that prepared heaven for you, shall prepare you to inherit that blessed place!'

"When Christ ascended, he found heaven plagued with devils; but, when you ascend, you shall find heaven cleansed of evil spirits. When we have got ready for translation, Christ will not tarry long.—Yours, in the Lord, HUGH WHITE."

In a note to this communication, Andrew Innes says—"This letter gives a true description of the faith and hope of the society at the time it was written. All our hopes were expected to be realized, with the same confidence that the disciples of Jesus expected to gain the promised land of Canaan before his death and burial. Their hopes were founded on the prophecies of the Old Testament; so were our hopes of personal translation without death; and we were confident that all the plagues mentioned in the Revelation of St John, would be poured upon our enemies, for the Lord says—"I will be an enemy to thine enemies, and an adversary to thine adversaries." [1]

The letter of Mr White to Thomas Bradley, had evidently the intended effect of hurrying him, and others in that quarter, to New Cample; but the words of Andrew Innes will best describe the progress of his mission in England. "After we arrived

[1] Exodus, xxiii 22

at Mr Bradley's house, we were mostly employed in reading the correspondence of Friend Mother, and the hymns and divine poems composed by Mr White, to the neighbours who called daily. Mrs Bradley expressed her desire to be at the society, with her family of six young children; and wanted two women of the society to assist her with them on the road; so Duncan went back to inform our Friend of this request. When Thomas Bradley's friends found that he was fully resolved to depart, they came often to persuade him of his folly, as they called it; and those who were sponsors for his children, threatened to detain them.

"One day as we were sitting in the kitchen with several neighbours, in comes a well-dressed man with a whip in his hand, and as if he had been driving a waggon, and attacked Thomas for his folly in proposing to leave a good farm, to go with his family to join a parcel of Scotch beggars, who would send him back to beg as soon as his money was spent. Thomas listened without saying much, then the stranger, looking to me, said, 'Who is this fellow?' Thomas replied, 'It is one of the society I am about to join.' He then raised his whip, and laid the but-end on my shoulders with all the force in his power, several times, and ordered me to begone. I rose, and was stepping towards the back door, when I received another stroke to quicken my pace, and, following me into the court-yard, he ordered me to depart immediately, lashing my legs all the time. Thomas was a quiet man, but by this time he was quickened, and, laying hold of his cousin, ordered him to leave the house, which he did, and I went back. But his cousin went to a justice of the peace, to take Thomas before him to be examined, and to get me sent out of the place as a vagrant.

"Next day a constable appeared, with a warrant for that purpose. Thomas saddled his horse, and I rode behind him to Sedgefield, and we were conducted into a room where there were two justices, who, after attacking Thomas in the same strain as his cousin had done, and telling him that he and his family would become burdens to the parish, strove to prove him insane, but in that they completely failed. I was charged with having put Thomas's brain wrong, and the constable was enjoined to take me off as a vagrant next morning.

"When Mrs Bradley heard the sentence of the justices, she ordered her servants to prepare, with all possible speed, victuals for the journey; and they got a large waggon packed with boxes containing clothes of all descriptions, and the women and children placed on it before daylight, and we were all gone before any of the neighbours knew. The waggon, drawn by two strong horses, moved at the rate of about fifty miles a-day. We had some difficulty in finding quarters by the way, as our number in all amounted to sixteen persons, which, upon our arrival at New Cample, made a considerable addition to our society."

The arrival of these persons is thus pompously announced in the Divine Dictionary:—

"O world! world! world! for which I sigh, consider these writings as for eternity. The spirit that guides the pen that writes these lines, is a witness against you, if found wanting in the balance of the sanctuary; will these well-meant lines not induce you to consider the momentous point of which they treat? Some people of good substance in England, have left all to come to this place, to wait with us and to hasten that blessed day of Christ's second coming."[1]

Many persons who were members of the society when in Irvine, but who did not choose to leave that place[2] at the time others did so, to follow Mrs Buchan, now left their homes under the assurance, that the great event so ardently wished for was at hand. The number now located in the small thatched house called "Buchan Ha,'" was upwards of sixty. Lest, in describing what follows, it might be supposed I wished to amuse the reader at the expense of truth, I will quote the words of Mr Innes:—

"We thought our hopes were about to be realized, when our landlord's sister came one morning very early, to inform us that the whole *onstead* of an adjoining farmer, named John Stitt, had been burnt to the ground, without any one being able to form the most distant idea of the cause of it. Still, being one of the most violent enemies, we were all well pleased to hear the news of the disaster that had befallen him, as we considered it to be the com-

[1] Divine Dictionary, p 48. [2] Appendix, Note 3

mencement of the general judgment, that was about to fall on all who did not believe in the divine mission of the author of our community; and if longer time has been granted sinners to repent, they have not us to thank for it.

"One evening when we were as usual all employed, some in the garret, and many below, Friend Mother was in the kitchen surrounded by children, when, on a sudden, a loud voice was heard, as if from the clouds. The children, assisted by our great luminary, struck up the following hymn:—

> 'Oh! hasten translation, and come resurrection!
> Oh! hasten the coming of Christ in the air!'

All the members below, instantly started to their feet, and those in the garret hurried down as fast as they possibly could through the trapdoor; but it being about midnight, and there being no light in the house, Mr Hunter, in the agitation of the moment, and being a feeble old man, tumbled headlong down the trap-ladder, whilst striving to descend from the cockloft. In an instant, however, he bounded from the ground, and, with a voice as loud as a trumpet, joined in the general chorus of 'Hasten translation,' which every one in the house sung most vehemently. The bodily agitation became so great, with the clapping of hands and singing, that it is out of my power to convey a just idea, on paper, of the scene which it occasioned: every one thought the blessed moment was arrived; and every one singing, leaping, and clapping his hands, pressed forward to the kitchen, where Friend Mother sat with great composure, whilst her face shone so white with the glory of God, as to dazzle the sight of those who beheld it; and her raiment was as white as snow.

"The noise was so loud, that the neighbourhood was alarmed. Thomas Davidson, our landlord, came to our door like a man out of his senses; he rapped and called at the door, till he obtained admission; and he, too, squeezed into the kitchen, beseeching her to save him, and the multitude by whom the house was surrounded, from the pending destruction, which they apprehended was about to destroy the world. She told them to be of good cheer, for neither he nor any of his friends would suffer any damage that night, for she now saw her people were not sufficiently prepared for the mighty change which she intended them to undergo.

"As the light passed from her countenance, she called for a tobacco-pipe, and took a smoke; and, as the extraordinary agitation diminished, the people without dispersed quietly. How long the tumult lasted, I was not in a state of mind to recollect; but, I remember, when daylight appeared, of having seen the floor strewed with watches, gold rings, and a great number of trinkets, which had been, in the moment of expected translation, thrown away by the possessors, as useless in our expected country. We did so, because Elijah threw away his mantle, when he was, in like manner, about to ascend to heaven. My own watch was of the number. I never saw it more; but I afterwards learned that

John Gibson, our treasurer, had collected all the watches and jewellery then thrown away, and sold them in Dumfries.

" This was, to many, as convincing a proof of our Friend Mother being the divine person Mr White represented her to be, as the Jews had on Mount Sinai, or as Peter, James, and John had on Mount Tabor, or as Moses gave the Israelites proof of his authority for bringing them into the fulfilment of the promise made to Abraham. We were now in the position of the apostles on the day of Pentecost, and with feelings nearly the same. It was only those that were near her, with their faces towards her, that could observe the change. It was with us, as it was with Paul's conversion—although all felt the power, all did not see the supernatural light; so, all did not hear the voice; and that may account for the division which afterwards took place among us.

" But this disclosure," continues Andrew, " was not like what is called the spiritual manifestations of the Quakers, Methodists, Rowites, Irvingites, or like the religious revivals at Kilsyth and other places, which all proceed from the same deceptive fountain. Their joy, or enlivening of their mind, arises from a hope in a God of whom they know nothing, yet whom they believe to be every where present, without a person or personal parts; and who, they believe, respects a soul which they suppose themselves to possess, which is composed of nothing, or is immaterial, which is the same, and without personal parts also, either to enjoy or to be enjoyed. Yet they solicit their unknown God to make their unknown souls happy through all eternity, in a place they know not where; yet it is in such a foundation all their faith and hope rest, from whence their joy arises. The hell they fall into, when this foundationless faith and hope gives way, is to be with the devil and his angels; but where that is, or if it is immaterial, I suppose many Protestants have yet to learn, or rather to make, before it can be discovered.

" The objects that enlivened our minds were all of a substantial quality, and all enjoyable by our senses; we expected to hear and see a God, such as Moses saw and heard from Mount Sinai; and a Jesus Christ, such as the three disciples saw on Mount Tabor; with a disposition of mind and manners, such as we saw and heard daily in their disguised representation. The woman clothed with the sun, and the moon under her feet, and her head ornamented with the likeness of Christ and his twelve apostles: whose light appeared in the words from her mouth, and his actions in the looks from her eyes; in all and every thing resembling Christ and his apostles, and, with such a companion to introduce us to the Holy of Holies, our confidence was great, and how could it be otherwise ?"

Such is the account given by Andrew Innes, of what he calls " The midnight manifestation." Though this wild scheme was thwarted solely by the established laws of nature, Luckie, as better answering her purpose, ascribed it wholly to want of faith in her followers, who, consequently, not having obtained the spiritual state necessary to their translation without tasting death, a total abstinence from all earthly nourishment for forty days, was deemed by her indispensably necessary to prepare those who should wish to profit by that great event. Elijah fasted forty days before his translation;[1] and Moses fasted forty days and forty nights in the presence of the Lord;[2] and Jesus remained forty days in the wildernesss, in a state of fasting;[3] and, finally, Peter, James, and John, needed no terrestrial support on the Mount of Transfiguration with God.[4] She likewise assured them, at the same time, that, as the blood receded from their veins, the Holy Spirit would occupy its place, and that they would consequently become spiritual bodies, like the great founder of their society.

If this proposal was made, as was generally supposed at the time by the people in that neighbourhood, only to frighten away many, who, it was feared, having nothing to support themselves, had joined the society merely for the sake of leading an idle life, the stratagem did not succeed, for all were alike enthusiastic.

[1] " And he (Elijah) arose, and did eat and drink, and went in the strength of that meat forty days and forty nights unto Horeb the Mount of God.' —1 Kings, xix. 8.

[2] " And Moses was in the Mount (Sinai) forty days and forty nights "—Exodus, xxiv. 18.

[3] Jesus, being forty days tempted by the devil, did eat nothing — Luke, iv. 1

[4] Matthew, xvii 1, 2

Mercy gave the word, and the great demonstration commenced with the following hymn, composed for the occasion by Mr Whyte :—

> " On words of God his children feed;
> For little by the mouth they need.
> In bliss they feed, by words and sight,
> To all that's God's having just right.
> Here we live, and here we feed,
> On living words, nor much we need.
> To live with God's a noble life—
> For earthly food we know no strife.
> The more on living words we feed,
> The less of earthly food we need."

I again adopt the words of Andrew Innes:— " After the fast began, we had very little intercourse with strangers. The door was bolted, and the windows nailed down and screened, letting in light only sufficient to enable us to see to read, for that, and singing hymns composed for the occasion, was our sole exercise. We read and sang so loud, as often to surprise those without; for many people came to see us, and when they could not get admittance, they walked about and listened at the doors and windows before they went away; but we never heeded them, as we were looking for the great event which was to relieve us from our earthly bondage; so that we much resembled Jonah when wishing and watching for the destruction of Nineveh, lest the repentance of the people should prevent the threatened overthrow of that city, and thereby establish for him the character of a false prophet. He had no regard for the many thousands in the devoted city who were to suffer by the judgment; neither had we for the whole world. We wished as seriously to see the whole world consumed by fire, as he desired the destruction of Nineveh.

"We never went to bed; some stretched themselves on coverlets, by turns, on the floor. The infirm generally lay couchant on the beds in the cockloft; and, it being about the middle of June, we scarcely knew night from day. When the fast commenced, we had twenty Scots pints, *i.e.* eight gallons, of molasses, a little manna, and a few stones of oatmeal in the store; but during the whole six weeks of the fast, there was no such thing as cooking victuals, and no complaint was made for want of food even by the children. There was, indeed, sometimes a desire for a little drink, and as Friend Mother was always stepping about among us, she kept a little treacle mixed with hot water, and allowed to cool, which she gave to any person who was thirsty; but it was very seldom required, except by a blind woman, who lay in bed the most of the time; and, as she was very deaf, and could not feed by the eye and the ear, as the rest of us did, she therefore required some earthly nourishment.

"Speaking from my own feelings, (and I have heard other persons say the same,) every desire for earthly food was taken away, and its place was supplied by a loathing at the thought of it. We were afraid of being disturbed by our neighbours before the forty days were expired, and therefore compelled to eat. These were not the figments of imagination, for we were supported without earthly food at this time, as the Jews were on manna in the desert; and we knew, as well as they did, that our support was derived from heaven, for, and by, the author of our Society."[1]

After the commencement of the fast, all the children, who still continued to be separated as much as possible from their parents, were surprisingly abstemious from food; so much so, that Mrs Hunter became so alarmed that her son and daughter, and even her husband, would be starved to death before the end of the forty days, that she communicated her fears to her friends in Irvine. Mrs Young, a sister of Mr H., was, in consequence of this communication, prevailed on to visit them at New

---

[1] The spiritual manifestations of the Buchanites bore, in many particulars, a remarkable resemblance to a noted sect of enthusiasts, who appeared in Dauphiny in the year 1688. When an assembly was appointed, men, women, and children poured forth from the surrounding hamlets, crying for mercy till the hills rebounded with the sound—mercy being the burden of their songs. Their preaching was always concerning the second coming of Christ, which they affirmed was at hand, and which event, they said, would be preceded by signs and wonders in the heavens, and by a deluge of judgments on the wicked throughout the world—as famine, pestilence, earthquakes, darkness, and fire from heaven. That the exterminating angels should root out the tares, and there would only remain on the earth good corn. Three of these visionaries came into England, and made many converts, the chief of whom was John Lacy, who wrote much on the subject of his divine mission. He concludes the preface to his "Last Warning," with these words,—"If, within six months now to come, the word of God doth not attest that we are from Him, I shall, before all the world, acknowledge my delusion. Witness my hand, this 29th day of October, 1707, John Lacy."—Edinburgh Christian Instructor, Appendix, Trial of Edward Irving, pp. 96, 97, 98, 99.

Cample, as being the most likely person to persuade her brother to return home; but, having failed in the object of her mission, Mrs Hunter formed the resolution of leaving Buchan Ha', with her sister-in-law, to try if she could, by legal means, remove her children and husband from the perilous situation in which they were placed. "It cost her little trouble," says Innes, "to make all our neighbours in the country, and even Sir James Kirkpatrick himself, believe that we were really insane by attempting to live without food, thereby opening the door to all the troubles that afterwards befell the Society."

The step taken by Mrs Hunter raised such a commotion in Buchan Ha', that the "Lady of Light" opened her spiritual artillery, in full force, on the offending female.

To Elizabeth Frances.

"New Cample, July 1786.

"MADAM,

"I, whom your person by faith once knew, have not forgot how you rejoiced therein; and now I, and all in heaven above, and all on earth below, know that you have not forgot in fear what you once minded in love; but let me, in God's great name, for whose name's sake you and this great world hate me, warn you, that your present pride shall in a little be turned into a stumbling-block and a pit of deep despair, for your conduct to ' the *people of God*, and your despite to the *Spirit of Grace*.' You have done as much evil as you could, though not one thousandth part of what you would like to do. Please remember you have condemned the just, and have not ceased to kill the precious faith, because the devil that is in you is aware, that it does not consist with the present dispensation to kill people for their faith, and this fills your heart with wrath. You have acted as a very bold champion, both in pride and malice; the devil has shielded and harnessed you with all the cunning of a serpent, and the deceit of a devil. Your unruly tongue has gone to the utmost of its power, though not the length of its will, to set all nature on hell's fire against ' the light and love of God,' who, in God's strength, was very active at that time in the great work for which it was sent to this nether world. But Christ shall come in flaming fire to take vengeance on all his enemies, and that fire shall take the flesh from their bones, and shall form it into the likeness of that foul fiend that it came from, and it shall have one lot and one portion with the devil for ever and ever, where the worm dieth not, and the fire is never quenched.

"I know that this is a discovery, that none of those in the world will like to hear of, but they shall hear of it, and, in due time, shall feel it, and that throughout eternity. Methinks, reflection on this, would make you cease to pervert the ways of the living God. If, at least, you will continue to sin against *Light* and *Love*, cease to be a *Hymeneus* and *Philetus* to others. I do not wonder that such a valiant soldier as you have been in the service of the devil, should be loath to lay down your weapon and armour of rebellion against the Most High, and, far less, to resign your commission; but you will only get a second death for your service, for the end of all the devil's subjects is to be burned.

"ELSPATH SIMPSON." [1]

As the faith of her followers declined, she greatly increased the extravagance of her pretensions, and the rigour of her discipline. Any person suspected of having an intention of leaving the society, was

---

[1] MS Letter-book. The following extract of a letter from Robert Montgomerie, Esq., banker, Irvine, alludes directly to the cause of Mrs Hunter's departure from the society, at the time of the Great Fast, though written sixty years after that period

"Irvine, 16th Feb. 1846.

" . . . Mrs Hunter was a very clever woman I have heard from what I considered very good authority, that the first thing that opened her eyes as to the character acted by Luckie Buchan, was a proposal made by her to Mrs Hunter to put her youngest child to death, as she said the child had the spirit of the devil in it "

I have received another equally important and authentic document on this subject, from Mr Alexander Hunter, a very respectable man, formerly farmer of New Cample, but now of Penpont

"Penpont, 19th July 1846.

" About twelve years ago, when sinking the foundation of a sty in the ruins of one of the old Buchanite houses at New Cample, I turned up, with my spade, the skull of an infant nearly entire The neighbours, who saw it, said many others had been raised near the same spot shortly before I came to live at New Cample; and at a subsequent period a great number of small bones were raised there "

It may be here stated that the crime of infanticide is vindicated under the general title of "Concerning propagation of the human race."—Divine Dictionary, page 14

locked up, and every day ducked in cold water;[1] but Mrs Hunter having been the first, of course escaped this penance, and, in spite of the preceding anathema, made her complaint, in a formal manner, to Sir James Kirkpatrick, one of the magistrates of the county of Dumfries, who granted a warrant to bring Mr Hunter and his children before a court at Brownhill, for the purpose of being examined on the points complained of by the petitioner.

Drs Yourstoun and Stewart, two eminent medical practitioners in the neighbourhood, being in attendance, examined Mrs Hunter's children, who, although reduced to skeletons by not having partaken food for nearly a month, refused every kind of nourishment that was offered to them; even sweetmeats, when put into their mouths, they rejected with seeming disgust, which very much surprised all the justices and attendants in court. They were, however, at length prevailed upon by their mother to partake of some refreshment with her. The elder of these children was a boy about ten years of age; the other, a girl two years younger.

The examination of Mr Hunter occupies several pages of the Innes MS. It is in substance a charge against Mr Hunter, by the court, of folly and ill-behaviour, in having left a good property and an excellent business, for the purpose of following a filthy, lascivious witch, to the ultimate ruin of his family. " Mr Hunter, being a lawyer, turned upon

[1] Sketch of the Life of Mrs Buchan Chambers' Biographical Dictionary, vol i p 386.

them like a lioness that had been robbed of its whelps, as to their right of interfering with his conduct in such a way;" but the proceedings were cut short by the production of a warrant from Irvine, under the authority of which Mr Hunter was escorted back to his native burgh, and was so strictly watched there afterwards by his friends, that no member of the Buchanite society was permitted to visit him, nor a letter from any of them to reach his hands.

The success of Mrs Hunter in recovering her husband and children from the Buchanites, not by charm, as people of yore were wont to recover their relations from the fairies, but by the force of law, induced Christian Clement, the mother of all the Inneses at New Cample, to follow a similar course. She found her son Andrew absent, as will afterwards appear; but the other members of the family were still under the wings of Mercy at Buchan Ha'. On being brought before Sir James Kirkpatrick, James and Margaret Innes agreed to return with their mother to Muthill, but Joseph refused to leave Mother Buchan. On being interrogated by Sir James how long he had been without food or nourishment of any kind, he replied, "If the stoutest man in the parish of Closeburn, not connected with the society, had wanted food for half the time I have done, he would have died ere now;" and, on being further interrogated, he said, that "he had not seen food of any kind cooked in the society for several weeks;"—a statement which partly corresponds with that of Andrew, his brother, in the narrative before me, who says, that "during the first four weeks of the Fast, there was not as much solid food consumed by all the members of the society, as he had seen one individual take at a single meal."

Under these circumstances, it occurred to the magistrates that there might have been some person starved to death at Buchan Ha', and their remains concealed there, particularly as the Buchanites were accused in the country of committing infanticide to a horrible extent.[1] They issued a warrant authorizing the premises to be strictly searched, which was immediately carried into effect by a posse of constables, who stated in their report, "that they could not find the remains of any person who might have been starved to death, or of any child who had been murdered."

Though no discovery was made on this survey, tending to criminate any individual member of the society, or even to strengthen the suspicions generally entertained of the unlawful practices of the body at large, yet that most revolting charge made against them by the public was not removed; it being, as already stated, one of their avowed dogmas, that the law which finished the bestial sacrifices at the altar, put an end to carnal marriages; and that, the unrestrained intercourse of the sexes was permitted by the inspired writers of the Old Testament.[2]

---

[1] Castle-Douglas Miscellany for 20th February 1846. Reminiscences of Mrs Black of Tinwald Shaws.
[2] Divine Dictionary, p. 71.

Mrs Buchan's sentiments on matrimony, are fully described by her in the following letter to a poor woman, who, it appears, was ruined by her husband having joined the Buchanites.

To Mrs James Brown, Sunderland.

"New Cample, June 1786

" MY DEAR,

"I will not return railing for railing, for I pity you. You wrote me, that James Brown had been your husband for twenty years. Alas! poor woman —did you see that bond in the light in which it is seen by God's love, you would have little to boast of. It is an agreement with hell and with death, and such bands are not to be boasted of; neither are such chains to be loved, and yet this boasting and love is most common in the world; but let me inform you, that these agreements with hell and with death shall be broken, for they were made to keep God's creatures in the bondage of corruption. This world has groaned under the bondage of what they call matrimony, since Adam and Eve believed lies of God, and became thieves. But the world shall be delivered from that accursed yoke by the people of God. . . . . . ELSPATH SIMPSON."

The propagation of dogmas so opposed to all the fundamental rules of the Christian Church, confirmed the religious people of Nithsdale in the belief, that the Buchanites were just a horde of incarnate devils, convened under a cloak of religion, merely to gratify reprehensible desires, accompanied by the revolting crime thus described by a poetaster of the day,—

> "But lest the gang should come to scorn,
> Whene'er an infant it was born,
> They threw it in the fire." [1]

A circumstance occurred at this time, calculated to strengthen this unfavourable popular belief. Katherine Gardner, who, previous to the formation of the society, had been housemaid in Mr Hunter's family, left Buchan Ha' with her old mistress, to resume her former station; but, finding herself pregnant to Andrew Innes, by the advice of her mistress and other friends, she speedily returned to New Cample to enforce her claim against him by law, lest he might be famished before the end of the Fast of Forty Days. When this case became known, it was fixed on by the public as an instance of incontinence, which would never have been known beyond the walls of Buchan Ha', had not the accidental circumstance just described led to its discovery.[2]

So strong was the excitement of the populace on this occasion, that it was deemed necessary, for the peace of the society, to send Andrew Innes away by night, lest he might fall a sacrifice to the fury of the inhabitants of Nithsdale. His own words, in

---

[1] "The Buchanites," a poem, by Henry M'Dowal, published 1792. Stanza ix.

[2] "These things excited much noise in the country side Many scandalous stories spread to their hurt. Their denial of marriage as an ordinance of heaven, led to reports of the grossest kind."—Struthers' History of the Relief Church, p 344.

describing the event, are—" Although our Friend Mother did all she could to prevent this, the voice of the whole society was against her. I was doomed to be cast out, like the man who had not the wedding garment. Mr White gave me five shillings, to bear my expenses home to Muthill, saying, that I was not to return without bringing with me a certificate from the minister of the parish, that I had recovered from my present deranged and confused state of mind, and that the society would receive no more trouble from Katherine Gardner on my account.

"Being more reduced in body than any other person in the house, by reason of the long fast, it became necessary to send me away on horseback, as I could not walk across the floor without the aid of a staff; so next morning, by cock-crow, they had me mounted on our landlord's old mare behind William Lindsay, and, accompanied by John Gibson on foot, we were past Thornhill before any of our enemies were out of bed to give the alarm. I suffered so much pain from being seated on the back of this jaded *garron*, that when I arrived at Leadhills, I could not alight of my own accord. John Gibson, therefore, lifted me off the horse in his arms, and carried me into the public-house, at the door of which we had stopped. Before parting with me there, they both partook of meat and drink, which surprised me very much, as I had seen nothing of the kind since the commencement of the Fast.

" Being very weak, I went to bed; and, after

getting a good sleep, and drinking some milk new from the cow, I found myself so far recovered next morning, as to be able to resume my journey. When I was about to depart, the mistress of the house informed me of the unsuitableness of my clothes to my person, especially my *breeks*, which, she said, had evidently been made for a much larger person, a thing I had taken no notice of. She gave me a needle and thread, to bring the waistband closer to my body, to relieve my hand from holding them up when I walked.

" There had been such a hurry at New Cample, to get me away in the morning before daybreak, that they had crammed me into the clothes that came first to hand, without regard to size or texture. My jacket was so tattered, and my hat so mis-shapen, that I must have had very much the appearance of a scarecrow; but my mind was too much occupied at the time with other matters, to mind what they did with me. When I had paid for my night's lodging, and the little refreshment I had received, the gudeman, perceiving my weakly state, kindly handed me a staff, leaning on which I stepped slowly to the door, and moved on the road as well as I could towards Douglas Mill; but, finding my strength failing, I lay down in an old quarry till I should recover a little, wishing, like Job, that I had never been born. After lying some time in a slumbering state, I was roused by the croaking of a flock of *corbie crows*, hovering just over me and making a great noise. Thinking they were come to pick out my eyes before I was dead, I turned my face to the ground to prevent them; but I expected every moment, as Peter the Apostle has described in his Second Epistle General, chap. iii. ver. 10, "to see the heavens pass away with a great noise, and the elements melt with fervent heat," and all the inhabitants destroyed, except the saints at New Cample, who alone were to be translated above the power of that great event, but from whom I had been unfortunately separated, and would, on that account, be one of the victims. I had, therefore, sufficient reason to be troubled, both in body and mind, for, ill-prepared as I was for that event, I may add, few in the hour were much better, *if little children were excepted*.

" While lying there. I had as convincing a proof, in a vision, that our Friend Mother was what Mr White represented her to be in his Divine Dictionary, as the shepherds who were watching their flocks by night at Bethlehem had, that the babe that was newly born there, and was lying in a manger, was the Saviour of the world. This heavenly disclosure not only enabled me to rise and accomplish my journey to Muthill, but it has enabled me to contend against the opposition by which I have been since assailed in my journey through life."

Although it was one of Mrs Buchan's original dogmas, that she was to wait with her flock till the second coming of Christ, yet, having taken upon herself the personification of the incomprehensible woman described in the Revelation of St John, and typically held her abode in the wilderness, she now found it necessary, before the expiry of the Fast of Forty days, to satisfy her adherents by giving an unequivocal proof of her divine mission. Mr Innes says—"Mr White wrote several poems in full confirmation of personal translation, which greatly increased our confidence in the fulfilment of that great event. Any attempt on the part of our Friend Mother at that time, to let us see our ill-prepared state for the reception of what we so anxiously expected, and supposed we were entitled to receive for our attachment to her, would have been very ill received." We here leave Andrew to wend his way to Perthshire, in his misfitted habiliments, while we glance at the strange events passing at New Cample.

There was a small green hillock immediately behind Buchan Ha', on the summit of which the whole knot generally assembled a few minutes before sunset, where they sung with such united strength, that the deeply mixed melody of their voices was frequently heard at Closeburn Castle, a mile distant. The swarm then returned to the hive; but on the evening in question they remained on the green knoll till midnight, and then moved off slowly towards Templand Hill,[1] which they ascended before the break of day, holding there what they called a Love Meeting—a term since used by the Methodists and Moravians.

According to the communication which I received

---

[1] Letter from Mr Lawrie, Tinwald Shaws

from the Rev. D. Mundell, rector of Wallace Hall Academy, dated 29th August 1839, they attempted to ascend in a body from Templand Hill at sunrise, which statement is further corroborated by another aged gentleman, Mr James Hossack, then of Thornhill, and latterly of Castle-Douglas. " I mounted my horse, and left Thornhill about sunrise, and as I was passing the farm of Templand, I was very much surprised at the sound of many voices in full chorus suddenly reaching my ears. The melodious strain came from the top of Templand Hill; and the silence of the scene, with the loneliness of the place, gave the music such a wildly impressive and mysterious effect, that I alighted from my horse, and, having tied it to a tree, I ascended the hill to ascertain if those sweet strains were really warbled from earthly lips, when, to my great surprise, I recognised several faces that I had seen at Buchan Ha', particularly that of Luckie Buchan herself. She was raised nearly her whole length above the crowd by whom she was surrounded, who stood with their faces towards the rising sun, and their arms extended upwards, as if about to clasp the great luminary as he rose above the horizon.[1]

[1] This singular meeting is thus described by John M'Taggart:— " At long and length the glorious day arrived, on which they were all to be taken to the regions above. Platforms were erected for them to wait on till the wonderful hour arrived, and Mrs Buchan's platform was exalted above all the others. The hair of each head was cut short, all but a tuft on the top, for the angels to catch by when drawing them up. The momentous hour came; every station for ascension was occupied; thus they expected every moment to be wafted into the land of bliss. A gust of wind came, but, instead of wafting them upwards,

"On a sudden the music ceased, and, being afraid I had been discovered by some of these enthusiasts, I hurried down the hill-side, mounted my horse, and rode on my way to Brownhill. On approaching that wayside inn, I was surprised to see the landlord and two strangers walking before the door at that early hour. After my horse was stabled, I went into the house with the host, and related to him my singular adventure on Templand Hill. Pointing to the persons still walking in front of the house, seemingly in great agitation, he said 'these men were also Buchanites, the one a farmer near Durham, and the other a tailor in Sunderland. They joined that sect only a few weeks ago, under the full assurance that they would, on their arrival at Buchan Ha', be wafted to heaven without tasting death. But it being required that they should fast for six weeks, to prepare them, like a horse in training,' they broke down when little more than half through, and have remained here since, to witness the result with those who would not relinquish till they had fasted the forty days as required. The persons you saw on the hill-top were the persons who had performed that extraordinary feat. As soon as the time of the

it capsized Mrs Buchan, platform and all! After this unexpected downcome, her words had not so much weight with them."—Gallovidian Encyclopedia, London, 1824, p 98 "So full was Mr White of the idea of his being carried aloft without tasting of death, that he dressed himself in his canonicals, put on his gloves, and walked about scanning the heavens. Crowds of country people were looking on, and expecting every minute that the sound of the archangel's trump would break upon their ears."—Struthers' Hist. of the Relief Church, p. 343.

great fast had expired, Luckie led her faithful followers forth to the hill, to take them thence direct to heaven, at sunrise this morning—if the strength or buoyancy of their faith be such as to lift their corporeal density. These two are now anxiously waiting to learn the result of these extraordinary proceedings, but I have heard both of them frequently express strong doubts as to the truth of Mrs Buchan's pretensions.'

"A sentinel, who had been stationed for the purpose of bringing, with all possible speed, intelligence of the first upward or downward movement of the people on the hill to the anxious expectants, soon came running in breathless haste with the news, that Luckie and the whole band were on their way back to New Cample. We all hastened to see them retrace their steps to their wonted abode; and such a company of half-famished looking creatures I never saw before. They were all deadly pale, and emaciated to the last degree; they seemed like living skeletons just eloped from the grave, or newly imported from Ezekiel's valley of dry bones, (Book of the prophet Ezekiel, chap. xxxvii;) with the exception of Luckie herself. She was like one of those beauties who crowd the canvass of painters with hillocks of rosy flesh. Her hair was unbound, and hung profusely over her back and shoulders. She was downcast and melancholy, as were all her followers, evidently from the exposure of their reckless folly. But the Fast of Forty Days could not have any effect upon the personal appearance of Mrs Buchan.

Unlike the ordinary mortals by whom she was surrounded—who abstained from food that they might thereby become pure inhabitants of the celestial kingdom—being a partaker of the Divine nature, she said she partook of earthly sustenance during the fast, as she did at other times, merely to prevent her tabernacle becoming too transparent for human eyes to behold, and took as her authority the following passages of Scripture:—" Then went up Moses into the ark with Aaron, Nadab and Abihu . . . . and they saw the God of Israel, and as it were the body of heaven in his clearness . . . . The sight of the glory of the Lord, was like devouring fire on the top of the mount in the eyes of the children of Israel." [1]

Such, then, was the termination of the great event set forth in the Divine Dictionary, and so confidently expected by every member of the society to be just at hand. Andrew Innes accounts for the failure, by observing that " she was under the necessity of doing with us, as Jesus did with his disciples, Peter, James and John, when they would not be satisfied without a sight of his Father. He ascended with them to the top of the mount, and allowed them to be sensible of their unfitness to receive what they so much desired. The same was it with us at Closeburn, at the conclusion of the Fast."

How different is the strain of the following extract from a letter, which I received from the only other male actor in the farce of " the Fast of Forty Days" now living, (1841.) The former writer,

[1] Exodus, xxiv.

affirms the heroine of that drama to have acted under the immediate and special direction of the omnipotent Ruler of the universe; while the following asserts, with equal confidence, that she was prompted by the arch-enemy of mankind :—

"Wolviston, 5th October 1840
"SIR,
"I received yours of the 19th August in due course, and, from the respectful manner in which it is written, I would be wanting in common civility were I not to give you all the information required in that letter, so far as it is in my power; but I was then in the midst of my harvest, and the subject on which you wished the information being long gone by, although I remember many circumstances well, I found it required a little time for consideration, to give you a correct answer, and I wished to see some of my sisters, they being older than I, and, as I thought, could recollect some points better.

"That my father and his family, of whom I am one, was at New Cample with the Buchanites, at the time you mention, is quite correct. He was sadly deluded by them, and plundered, under the garb of religion, or rather, I should say, under the most romantic enthusiasm imaginable. With regard to all their religious tenets, I cannot enter into a minute detail of them in the compass of a letter; but the leading principles of them were, that none of them were ever to die, but were to be taken up direct to heaven; and all who were not of their party, were to be burnt up and destroyed.

"A night was fixed when time was to end, and when all these great events were to happen; but the morning came, and yet Mrs Buchan and all her followers remained at New Cample. She then told them, that the reason of all she had predicted that night not having taken place, was, because they were not ready for so great a change. That they therefore would require to fast forty days, to prepare them for the ascension or translation of each individual. Accordingly, the fast was proclaimed, and, as I believe, the most of them fasted the time, or nearly so. All were reduced to mere skeletons, with the exception of Mrs Buchan and Mr and Mrs White. I dare say they told their followers that they fasted also, and took care to let none see to the contrary; but their appearance spoke different, as they continued to look as well as ever.

"Her attempt to ascend to heaven was only of a piece with many other of her profane actions.[1] When they failed, she had a cunning knack of clearing herself, and of working on the feelings of her followers after such disappointments. It was always the weakness of their faith that caused the failure of what she had proposed to them. By such arts, she soon placed all right again on her part—I mean before the fast —for after that event she was not so successful. . .

[1] Letter from the Rev John Richmond, minister of Southdean, Roxburghshire

"I was one of the children that were taken from under the care of Mrs Buchan at the fast, as was my sister Mary, by the warrant of the magistrate. I was then ten years of age, and she was fourteen, but I stood the fast better than she did; for when taken out, she was nearly lifeless, and after getting food she grew quite delirious, and continued so for several weeks. She then got well, but for three years she had relapses of want of reason, for two or three weeks at a time, with intervals of three or four months between, when her reason returned. At the expiration of three years, she got quite well, and continued so for several years, was married, and had a family of six children. But her former complaint returned during her confinement of the last three; the last time, it finally terminated in her death in that state.

"This, sir, is a correct account of the Buchanites, so far as I can recollect, and a true description of my sister's case, which it has been painful to me to relate. How far it might or might not be attributable altogether to the fast as the cause, I must leave you to judge. There have been cases, certainly, where there have been nothing of the kind to ascribe as the cause; but her case was peculiarly pointed, and therefore the more affecting.—I remain, Sir, &c.,

(Signed) " THOMAS BRADLEY.

" To Mr Joseph Train."

The case of Mr Bradley's sister is one of a melancholy description, which, for the sake of humanity, we hope is of rare occurrence. To ascertain if the want of food at the age of fourteen years, was the cause of the intermittent malady, which terminated in her death so many years after the time of its commencement, might be a question for the most learned of the medical faculty to solve. Certain it is, the delusive idea was entertained by several of the Buchanites, that to their being fed during the fast "by the eye and the ear by the Holy Spirit," which they supposed Mrs Buchan to possess, was to be ascribed the preservation of life for a greater length of time than would have otherwise been the case, in the absence of all earthly aliment.

It was, indeed, as Mr Bradley terms it, " a most romantic enthusiasm," which could induce a body of men to undergo such privations, in the vain hope of obtaining an object, improbable to all but the most diseased understanding; and yet not the least remarkable feature of the case was, the permanency of its hold on the minds of many of the poor dupes to the last.

CHAPTER IV.

Many of the disappointed expectants of immortality become disaffected—Luckie and her coadjutor committed to prison—Subsequently tried by the kirk-session of Closeburn for criminal conversation—Retrospective account of Andrew Innes—He returns with his wife and infant daughter to the society—The Buchanites banished from Dumfries-shire—Their arrival and residence at Tarbreach, in Galloway—They remove to Auchengibbert, where they work for wages—Singular instance of their superstitious veneration for the founder of their sect—Credulous account of her culinary powers—Many of the members of the society become disaffected and unruly—Mother Buchan complains of their backsliding—She is not allowed by Mr White to go from home, nor permitted to speak to strangers on religious topics—Her last illness—Commotion caused by her death—That she visibly ascended to heaven, affirmed by those who watched her corpse by night—The place of her interment consequently concealed—Parallel between her and Mother Lee

Many of Luckie's followers having now become doubtful as to the reality of her pretensions, the persons who did so she declared to be possessed by an unclean spirit, which she pretended to cast out, individually, by a ceremony too rude to meet the eye or ear of modesty; and few submitted to her purifying ordeal.

The people from England, who joined the Buchanites, had all, with the exception of Conyers, been of the Methodist persuasion, and were governed by a belief that they had been sanctified before they saw Mrs Buchan, and only wanted glorification by her. Their expectations, in this respect, being ended with the fast, they immediately became her accusers for deceiving them with vain hopes. Many of them having placed all their worldly means at the disposal of the society, now actually became common beggars. Ashamed to return to their homes, they went from door to door throughout the greater part of Scotland, depicting, in unmeasured terms, the darker shades of Luckie Buchan's character, and detailing the miseries they had brought upon themselves and their families, by listening to her irreligious fooleries.

The most violent of these was James Brown, the tailor from Sunderland; but several of the Irvine people acted in a similar manner. Mr Chambers says, " In the year 1786, the following facts were reported by some of the seceding members, on their return to the west:—The society being once scarce of money, she informed them that she had a revelation, informing her that they would have a supply of cash from heaven; accordingly, she took one of the members out with her to the summit of a neighbouring hill, and caused him to hold two corners of a sheet extended, while she held the other two. Having continued a considerable time in that position, without any money falling from heaven, the man at last tired, and left Mrs Buchan to hold the sheet herself. In a short time afterwards, she returned with five pounds, and upbraided the man for his unbelief, which, she said, was the cause which prevented it from coming sooner. Many of the members easily accounted for the pretended miracle, and shrewdly suspected that the money came from some hoard."[1]

When Mr Hunter left the society, he gave a free discharge for all the money he had expended for the use of its members, although that sum amounted to nearly three hundred pounds; but John Gibson, one of those who were about to return to Irvine, acted in quite a different manner. He made a charge of eighty-five pounds, which was refused by Mr White. But "Gibson being our treasurer," says Andrew Innes, "knew what money he had left in the box, and therefore came slyly back, accompanied by Stewart, who had left us also, in the hope of getting hold of it; but Mr White, suspecting that such an attempt might be made, removed the money, so that they found nothing but the empty box."

On finding his scheme thus frustrated, Gibson made out a detailed account of his claim, and obtained a fugie warrant against Mr White and Mrs Buchan, who were apprehended and laid in Dumfries jail. The greater part of those members who had broken down under the protracted fast, as before mentioned, lingered in the neighbourhood, either to witness the grand translation, or final dispersion of the remaining expectants of immortality. Thomas Bradley, one of the number, who, like Ananias, on selling his lands, kept part of the proceeds to himself, and only gave a part to the "community

[1] Biographical Dictionary, vol i. p 386.

of goods," generously stepped forward without any solicitation, and lodged the sum demanded by Gibson, as well as by some others who had followed his example, to the amount of one hundred and seven pounds, in the hands of Mr Short, town-clerk in Dumfries, by way of bail, until the validity of the claims should be decided in due course of law, thereby obtaining the liberation of his former friends.[1]

This disinterested act of kindness was shamefully abused by the parties most interested. Mr White, following the example set by Gibson, preferred a charge against Thomas Bradley for the sum of eighty-five pounds, as board wages for himself and family during the short time they were with the society, and, with a view to secure payment, arrested the money lodged by him in the hands of Mr Short. Having joined the Buchanites unconditionally, Mr Bradley refused to pay this unreasonable demand, but, having removed to England with his family, without employing any one to attend to his interests, White, on 1st February 1787, obtained a decreet from the sheriff of Dumfries-shire against Thomas Bradley, then of Foggytower, in the county of Durham, for the sum of £53, 16s., as the balance of a particular account contracted by him with the Buchanites, as libelled upon and produced.[2]

It would have been no worse for Thomas Bradley, had the decreet covered the whole sum deposited by

[1] Appendix, Note 5.
[2] Records of the Sheriff Court of Dumfries-shire.

him in Mr Short's hands, as he never received a penny of the balance. In a letter from White to Mr Bradley, dated "*Auchengibbert, 25th March* 1791," he says, "The greedy lawyers in Dumfries never mean to part with the money lodged in Mr Short's hands, if possibly they can keep it. Mr Short has had it so long, that he now looks upon it as his own."

At the request of Mr Bradley's son, I lately endeavoured to ascertain what became of the balance between the sum deposited and that for which the decreet was granted, but the parties immediately concerned being all dead, I could obtain no satisfactory information on the subject.

According to Andrew Innes, the charge made by Mr White never had an existence in the society, nor was any part of the money received by him on that account, ever applied to their use.[1]

It having been proved to the satisfaction of John Welsh, Esq. of Milton, sheriff-substitute of Dumfriesshire, that Gibson had put his money voluntarily into the general purse of the society, his case was dismissed; but, while smarting under the issue of his fancied claim, he impeached Mr White and Mrs Buchan before the kirk-session of Closeburn, of having carried on an improper intercourse, to establish which charge, several of the disaffected members of the society were summoned as witnesses;[2] and so in-

[1] Letter, dated Crocketford, 29th November 1840.
[2] Reminiscences of Mrs Black, Tinwald Shaws.

tent was the anxiety of the people, that not only the whole neighbourhood, but many from a considerable distance, attended to hear the examination.

For the following extracts from the session books of the parish of Closeburn, on this subject, I am obliged to Dr Mundell of Wallace-hall Academy:—

"The Session, considering that this was a case which properly came under the cognisance of the presbytery in the first instance; they therefore referred it to the presbytery, to meet at Penpont on the 1st day of October 1786. The charge against the aforesaid parties came before the Presbytery of Penpont, by reference from the session of Closeburn, with the minutes wherein Gibson and others had libelled Mr White and Mrs Buchan, as already stated; but the pursuers not appearing, the case was dismissed.[1]

"The Session, however, having Mr White and Mrs Buchan before them, thought it incumbent upon them, as trustees for the poor and managers of the public funds of the parish, to put some questions to Mr White and Mrs Buchan with regard to the possibility of any of the members of their society becoming burdensome to the parish.

"*Question First*—What is the number of your society?

---

[1] Letter from Mr George Hunter, clerk of Penpont Presbytery, dated 8th May 1839.

"*Answer by both Mr White and Mrs Buchan*—We do not know.

"*Question Second*—Have the number of your society been changing since you came into this parish, some going away and others coming?

"*Answer*—Yes.

"*Question Third*—Have you any funds in the society for the support of the members?

"*Answer by Mr White and Mrs Buchan*—Some of the members of the society have money, which they freely apply to the use of the rest as occasion requires, but what the amount of the money is we do not know.

"*Question Fourth*—What reason can you give to make us believe that the members of your society who have money, whatever it be, will continue to apply it to the use of the rest?

"*Answer by Mr White and Mrs Buchan*—We are sure they will continue to relieve the wants of the rest so long as they will stay with us.

"*Question Fifth*—Is it contrary to the rules of your society to work for wages?

"*Answer by Mr White and Mrs Buchan*—They work, but never for wages.

"The sederunt then closed with prayer.

 (Signed) "ANDREW YORSTOUN, Moderator.

"Extracted from the record of the Session of the parish of Closeburn, this 14th day of August 1839, by THOMAS REDPATH, S.C."

Having placed the charges and particulars in the handwriting of Mr Thomas Redpath, clerk of the Closeburn session, and of Mr George Hunter, clerk to the presbytery of Penpont, in the hands of Andrew Innes, for his remarks thereon, he, in a communication which I received from him on the subject, after charging his mother, Christian Clement, with perjury, reluctantly admits, that "the fact of Mr White and Mrs Buchan sleeping in the same bed, was never intended to be kept a secret in the society; but it was never intended to have communicated it to any, who would have made it a stumbling-block or a rock to split on. Those, however, who became dissatisfied after the fast, considered it as a chief article to expose, because it was sure to obtain her condemnation in the world; but in the society, her trial by the Closeburn session was, to my knowledge, never mentioned after it was over."

Gibson returned to Irvine to resume his former occupation of a builder,[1] but his wife refused to accompany him, because, in his capacity of treasurer to the society, he, as she said, betrayed his mistress; thereby following the example of Judas, the treasurer of Jesus Christ, in betraying his master.

[1] "I have often heard my father mention, as a curious fact, that all those who had belonged to the Buchanites, after leaving them, entered into the Established church, though most of them had been Dissenters of various denominations before joining the prophetess, and embracing her tenets."—Letter, dated 12th Jan 1846, from the Rev. John Richmond, Southdean, Roxburghshire, son of the Rev. Dr Richmond, minister of Irvine when the Buchanites assembled there.

Whilst the inmates of Buchan Ha' were thus employed in settling disputes with rebellious and disaffected brethren, Andrew Innes, having escaped from the "Corbie Craws" at Leadhills, spent some time at Muthill, preparatory to his return to the society, which he thus describes:—

"When I arrived at Falkirk, on my way from New Cample to Muthill, I spent a day there, getting my clothes made suitable for my person. On reaching home, I took to my bed for two or three days, to avoid, as much as possible, the railing of my relations and friends who came to see me; several of whom came, I was quite aware, for the sole purpose of chiding me for what they were pleased to call my folly; but my sister's scolding was worst to bear. She said I had put my sister out of a comfortable way of making a livelihood, and had brought the family to poverty and disgrace.

"Drummond Castle being at that time in course of repairing, I rose and went there to try to procure employment, but not succeeding, I afterwards went to Crieff for the same purpose, but with no better success. My character as a Buchanite, made every person who could have done so, afraid to employ me. Every one turned away from me, as they would have done from a serpent, which made me think of returning to the society again. When my sister became aware of this, she became very angry, and advised me, instead of doing so, to go to Ayrshire and marry Katherine Gardner, and her relations would procure work for me. To this I at length agreed, upon her procuring me a certificate from the minister of the parish that I was a single man. Having no money to bear my expenses to Katherine Gardner's residence at Stevenston, all I got from my sister was as much cloth as would make two shirts, which I sold in Glasgow for six shillings. On arriving at Stevenston, I called on Katherine. She said her parents would prevent her returning with me to Closeburn, unless I would submit to the ceremony of marriage, to deprive them of the control over her. As I was aware that the most legal union that marriage could bind, would be done away on entering the society to which we were about to return, I agreed to the proposal; so we were proclaimed in the church, and married in her father's house by the parish minister. About this time, I received the following letter from our Friend Mother:—

"New Cample, 27th October 1786.

"My dear children, of whom I travail in birth till Christ has formed in you the hopes of glory. It is your act of faith that puts an end to all former unbelief. My friends, I am sure you have known the difference between the world's laws and the laws of God, more since you left this place, than you did when you were here; at least you might have done so. You should not have wearied in well-doing, for in good time you shall reap the benefit of it, if you faint not. What grief has God got in all dispensations, by fall of apostates from truth, I need not write much at present, as I hope to see you soon. I wrote Peter Hunter by James Innes, but have not received any answer. Try and call on him privately, before you come here. Your loving mother in the Lord, ELSPATH SIMPSON."[1]

"Katherine Gardner had a daughter about this time, and as soon as she could travel we returned to the society, and were kindly received by all, but by none more so than by Friend Mother herself, for she knew that we had committed no crime; there being in the society no separation of sexes.

"Katherine Gardner nursed her child for about eight months, when it was taken from her, and given to another woman. The child grew up, and lived in the society for twenty years, without knowing either the one or the other of her parents, so far as I ever heard or saw, although we were both there all the time; neither of us having been a night absent from her, from the time of her birth till the day of her death."

A person named Jasper Armstrong, who had been

[1] Note by Andrew Innes.—"This letter was written to me when I was in Stevenston on Katherine Gardner's business. She shows that we were the cause of leaving the society ourselves. Katherine left the society herself, but Mr White was the chief cause of sending me away. She expected an answer from Mr Hunter by my brother James, who was returning to the society; but we supposed the letter had never been delivered to him, as Mrs Hunter kept him so closely watched, that no person from the society was ever permitted to see him, nor any communication from it allowed to reach his hands

an apprentice to Duncan Robertson, one of the Buchanites, wrote a short sketch of the Buchanites, which appeared in the "Castle-Douglas Miscellany," published many years ago, in which he says—"This girl was the only offspring that ever saw the light among the Buchanites. She was never baptised, but they called her *Cintals,* and a curious, original-looking creature she was; she never was allowed to go anywhere from home; so that, beyond the bosom of their own community, the world and its contents were unknown to her."

Mr White was summoned to attend a court of county magistrates at Brownhill, in January 1787, to produce security that none of the society would become a burden on the parish, as they by law would have a claim for support, if permitted to remain a few months longer in the place.[1] The wealthy people having all left the society, and Mr White not being able to procure the security required, it was decreed that every member of the society located at New Cample, should leave Dumfries-shire on or before the tenth of March following.

In the language of Andrew Innes, "this was driving Friend Mother and her children into the wilderness a second time, with a worse prospect of support than when they were obliged to leave the town of Irvine in a similar manner." For several weeks afterwards, these unfortunates knew not where to steer in search of another domicile; but Thomas

[1] Reminiscences of Mrs Black of Tinwald Shaws

Davidson, their landlord, at length succeeded in obtaining for them a lease of Auchengibbert—a wild moorland farm of considerable extent, but then of little value, in the parish of Urr and stewartry of Kirkcudbright, from Mr John Bushby, sheriff-clerk of Dumfries-shire; and, in conjunction with Mr White and Mrs Buchan, became bound in the lease for the fulfilment of the terms specified in the engagement. Until they could obtain admittance to the farm at the ensuing Whitsunday, Mr Davidson procured for them the old mansion-house of Tarbreach, in the neighbourhood of Kirkpatrick-Durham.

These particulars being known only to the parties immediately concerned, as the time of their departure drew nigh, many persons came from Muthill, from Irvine, and even out of England, to witness, as they expected, the final dispersion of the society, and to take home, if possible, their friends and relations, who had continued to locate, up to that time, in New Cample. The Buchanites were much alarmed at this intelligence, being afraid of a convoy such as had attended them at Irvine. They procured horses and carts for the removing of their bedding and furniture from Mr Davidson;[1] and, having made

---

[1] Mr Davidson's death was singularly painful On travelling over Leadhills not many years ago, he was overtaken by a heavy fall of snow, and, losing his way, was exposed all night to the inclemency of the weather, which so affected his legs and feet that from his knees downwards the flesh mortified, and death speedily ensued. This unhappy circumstance appeared to his religious neighbours an evident manifestation of divine displeasure against him for having harboured such a band of unsanctified sinners as the Buchanites Mr Davidson, although very friendly to that sect, had never become a member of their society

all things ready for their departure, they moved off from New Cample in a body, at one o'clock in the morning of the 10th of March 1787. Mr White's poem, written on the occasion, shows that they did not escape quite unmolested.

> " The tenth day of March being closely impending,
> Like voracious hawks which the doves doth pursue,
> Or wolves which the sheep and the lambs doth devour still,
> Came Closeburn's people God's course to undo;
> The eyes of devourers at that hour all enter
> Where dwells God's bright Spirit, our motions to watch,
> That they might distress us in time of decampment,
> That they might conjointly mischief 'gainst us hatch.
>
> " The first who observed us ran bellowing loudly,
> The country alarming, till clusters combined;
> The hills and the valleys, the lawns and the highways,
> With people were crowded before and behind.
> Though tongues were quite lawless, their hands were confined,
> The light of the sun and the laws of the land
> These gazers deterred from using their violence,
> And thus we escaped from their wicked land."[1]

In a field adjoining the old mansion of Tarbreach, a kind of hustings was erected, from which Mrs Buchan and Mr White held forth on certain days to large assemblies of people, prompted by curiosity to come, frequently from a great distance, to hear these noted individuals, whose absurd tenets at this time were known and detested over the greater part of Scotland. As the novelty of these field meetings began to decrease, the number of attendants became less, till they were at length completely deserted,

---

[1] From the Buchanite Hymn-Book, pp. 28, 29,—" A most miserable collection of nonsensical rhymes," as they were termed by the poet Burns.—Cromek's Reliques, edit. 1813, p. 197.

save by the original members of the sect. They never made a convert in Galloway.

The Buchanites did not support themselves by preaching, as the pastors of most other sects do. Andrew Innes says, he never saw a collection of money attempted to be made by the society, either before or after service, if such it may be called, except once at Muthill, when Mr White preached there. Neither did they work for hire, as long as the means of the persons who joined them lasted. On taking possession of the farm of Auchengibbert, their funds were so far exhausted, that a shower of money would have been of real service to them there, but Mrs Buchan's success in this department appears to have left her.

At Auchengibbert, they had, as it were, to commence the world anew. "Our stock," says Andrew Innes, "consisted of only one cow, a calf, and two stirks, purchased on credit, with an old horse presented to us by our landlord at New Cample, and another brought from England by Thomas Bradley, and left with us at his departure. On account of our stock being so small, and our not having the means of enlarging it, we took in cattle to graze for payment. There being no houses on the farm, and our means having left us, I, with a few assistants, erected a stable and byre, and subsequently, whilst others made fences to confine the cattle, Duncan Robertson made spinning-wheels, and the women having soon got regular employment in spinning factory yarn at threepence per hank, we therewith obtained money to purchase potatoes and meal for food. In harvest we all went out to shear, at eightpence per day, with victuals. This was the first deviation from our original plan of working gratis to our neighbours; but necessity compelled us to do so, as, at our entering the farm, we had no more money than purchased three stones of oatmeal, which cost four shillings and sixpence.

"We had a tinsmith who made articles in his line for sale, which were carried into the moorlands by some of the women, and bartered for wool, which was very useful to us, as our wardrobe had become very scanty of both body and bed-clothes—those who left the society having taken with them all the spare clothing and bed-clothes. The wool was spun with all possible speed, and made into cloth—that for the men was made very stout, but that for the women of a slighter fabric. In a short time we all got dressed anew, in cloth of a light green colour.

"Mrs Muir, who had kept a cloth-shop in Irvine, had many articles of her stock remaining, which she carried about the country, and bartered for any thing that we were in need of. It was while thus employed, that Friend Mother wrote the following letter to her:—

"Auchengibbert, December 1779.

"My dear Child,

"The waters of life are running here clear as crystal; your brothers and sisters are longing much to see you. There is great reason to bless the almighty power of heaven, for bringing about and maintaining the peace we enjoy in this place; and, indeed, when I look back to the mighty power and holy skill of heaven attending us, we may sing and say, it is God that carries our expenses. . . . . —Yours, in the Lord,   ELSPATH SIMPSON."

"We were," continues my informant Andrew, "now all obliged to work for hire, though we were well aware it would be considered by those who left us, and by the world at large, as a direct contradiction of what Mr White had said and published in his works, and of what our Friend Mother had taught in nearly the same manner, as the apostles forbade circumcision and the other law ceremonies, after Pentecost. While in Irvine and in Closeburn, we were in daily expectation of personal translation, which caused us to care little for the world. Mr White then, in explaining Friend Mother's views of the Scriptures, distributed judgment without mercy or respect of persons, or without caring for the approbation or persecution of the world; but not so in Galloway: his hopes, to a certain extent, being disappointed, he knew we had to provide for the necessaries of life, and he therefore allowed us to work, and wished every member of the society to avoid conversing on religious topics, and did so himself, to prevent further persecution.

"George Hill frequently reeled the yarn spun by the women, and assisted them when working in the fields, as did Mr White; but his chief employment was writing poems in praise of Sir Alexander Gordon, sheriff of the county, and also of Dr Lamont, minister of Kirkpatrick-Durham, and Dr Muirhead, minister of the parish of Urr, who both paid us great attention,—the former, while we were at Tarbreach, the latter while we were at Auchengibbert." [1]

The rectitude, amiability, and benevolence of these gentlemen, individually, could not appear to greater advantage by being so lavishly bedaubed in the doggerel rhymes of Mr White. These productions were, however, excusable when viewed as the sentiments and feelings of their author and his associates, in appreciating the kind treatment they received at the hands of these gentlemen. The two latter, besides being ministers of the respective parishes in which they resided, were magistrates of the county also. When called upon by religious individuals to exercise their magisterial authority, by putting the Buchanites out of the country, as those in Dumfries-shire had done, they always replied, that "the visionary doctrines and enthusiastic notions contained in the theological system propagated by Mrs Buchan and her coadjutor Mr White, were too absurd to merit the slightest attention in a religious point of view; and as there was no danger of even the most ignorant of the multitude being now con-

---

[1] Dr Lamont thus speaks of the Buchanites when residing at Tarbreach—" Though a religious sect, called Buchanites, resided for some time in this parish, yet that circumstance did not produce one instance of apostacy from the established church. In short, the wildness and the bigotry of fanaticism, are giving place to liberal sentiments and rational religion."—Statistical Account of Scotland. Edinburgh edit 1792, vol. ii p 261.

taminated by their false views of the sacred Scriptures, their heresy, if allowed to pass undisturbed, would soon fall into merited obscurity, whereas every obstruction offered would have a contrary effect."

Dr Lamont having once called at Auchengibbert, Mrs Buchan, to show her gratitude, as she said, for his forbearance, as the minister of the parish, towards her children while they remained at Tarbreach, advanced towards him for the purpose of breathing on him the Spirit, or the Holy Ghost, which it is said she always did " with postures and practices that were scandalously indecent." The Doctor, though nearly taken, by surprise, rejected the proffered inspiration, and was so disgusted at this horrid blasphemy, that he instantly left the house, and never held any further communication with Mrs Buchan or any of her followers.

Dr Muirhead took many of his acquaintances to see the Buchanite establishment at Auchengibbert; but the indignant rejection made by his neighbour clergyman, of the spiritual honour intended to have been conferred on him, prevented the Doctor being troubled in like manner. Having landed property not far from Auchengibbert, the reverend gentleman employed several of the Buchanites during the first harvest after their arrival in his parish. A few days after the commencement of their labour, Mother Buchan went, as she said, " to see how her bairns were getting on with their work." The moment she entered the field where they were employed, they threw down their sickles, and, after embracing each other, moved towards her in a body, with their heads uncovered and their hands in a supplicating attitude. They also struck up, with a loud voice, to their favourite tune, "Beds of sweet roses," their hymn, beginning, "O hasten translation." As soon as the music met the ear of "the Lady of Light," she stopped, and, raising her hands and eyes towards heaven, stood in that position till they had formed a circle round her; then, uttering a short benediction, she placed the palm of her right hand on the head of a young man, who instantly fell prostrate on the ground as if deprived of life, with his face downward, and, in like manner, she laid her hand on the brow of every other individual in the circle with similar effect. Then, extending her arms and saying a few words, which every ear was raised a little from the ground to hear, and kneeling down, she again touched with the palm of her hand the forehead of each individual in succession, who immediately started up like an automaton figure, raised by the pressure of an internal spring. As soon as these singular devotees had attained an upright position, they embraced each other again. She moved slowly away in the midst of them, while they sung with great vehemence, to the amazement of the remaining reapers, this popular hymn:—

"Let no one imagine we here mean to tarry,
Although to the parish of Urr we have come;
By us Auchengibbert has only been taken
To rest in, as onward we march to our home."

"I recollect," says Andrew, "a circumstance which happened at Auchengibbert, immediately after James

Sanders joined us there. He heard others speak frequently of the happiness we had enjoyed during the fast of forty days, and supposed he never would be like them till he had fasted forty days also. From the circumstance of my being absent at the time, as already mentioned, I had not fasted the number of days required; so I agreed to join him in fasting, by ourselves, for that period, to prevent, as I thought, my being left behind those who had made out the full time, when the great day of our exaltation arrived; but some of the women, having got notice of our intention, informed Friend Mother, who immediately sent for us, and, addressing herself to me, said, I was like the Jews in the wilderness, who thought they could conquer their enemies and take possession of the holy city, without the help of Moses; but they no sooner made the attempt, than they were beaten back with the loss of many lives. She said, if I thought I could either perform a part of her work myself, or help her to do so, I would find myself unsuitable for either, and the only way I could assist her most was, not to interrupt her in the work she was sent to perform. She then turned to James Sanders, and said, he had nothing to fear from not having been present at the great fast; for the last person that joined her family would meet the same reward, if sincere, as those who thought they had borne the burden in the heat of the sun; so we thought no more of our intended fast.

"I also remember a reproof given by her to Mrs Gibson, about the same time, for a fault somewhat similar to mine. We were sitting on the grass one day before the door, when Mrs Gibson said—'O, Friend Mother, when will I be like you?' Her answer was—'To strive or seek to be like me, is to be like my greatest enemy. It was the angel's attempting to be like God that made him a devil, and it was the followers of the apostles seeking to make themselves like Christ that made them Antichristians.'

"I recollect also of her once asking James Sanders, if he did not think it was those persons whom she kept most in her company, and consulted in all she did, that were her best friends? He said, he thought they were. 'Then,' said she, 'you are wrong—they were quite the reverse. Those whom I can send to their work by the stamp of my foot, or a shake of my fist, might be an example to the others.' Though Mr White heard this without making any remark, he would very probably rebuke her in private for saying so, as the allusion was evidently levelled at him. Formerly, he received his instructions from her, like an obedient child from its mother; but in Auchengibbert he supposed himself qualified to be her instructor in spiritual things, and in worldly affairs also."

The next extract I am about to make from the MS. so often quoted in the course of this sketch, is very hard to believe :—

"Being greatly reduced in numbers, we had frequently much better accommodation at Auchengibbert than we had at New Cample, but for some time after we arrived at the former place, we got only two meals a day of very simple fare. Our diet, however, gradually increased both in quantity and quality as we could afford it.

"Our Friend Mother was always permitted to manage the cooking department, particularly in times of scarcity, as she always produced plenty of the most delicious food, from articles of the most simple description. Her works in the kitchen can only be described by those that enjoyed the production of them. No stranger can believe what large quantities of the most delicious food she presented on the table daily, to upwards of forty persons, from a very few potatoes or cabbage, with a few carrots or turnips, and a few handfuls of oat or barley meal. I had the charge of the stores; and I can affirm, that when she had charge of the kitchen, I only gave out one basinful of meal weekly, which was about a stone; whereas, when Mrs White or any of the women had charge of the cooking, I had to give out four or five times that quantity, and the same in the quantity of potatoes, with no perceptible difference at table.

"Mr Syme's cookmaid visited us frequently to see her child, that was kept for payment by Magdaline Gardner, and I heard her say that our Friend Mother could make more substantial and more palatable broth from a single spoonful of butter, or a few other materials of the simplest kind, than any other person could do with a whole joint of mutton, and plenty of vegetables of the best description."

From this display of the miraculous powers of Mrs Buchan, we must turn away dissatisfied as to its accuracy, on the general ground, that he who has been deceived himself, is pleased to see others deceived also. Alleged miracles have too frequently rested solely on the authority of those who might have invented such frauds, and who alone had the power to aid any enquiry tending to undeceive the believers in them.

Mr White, being tacksman of Auchengibbert in conjunction with Mr Davidson, directed the labour of the various individuals located there in the way most likely to meet the demands of the landlord, and was himself both purveyor and treasurer; but it appears they soon became dissatisfied with his management. " His inclination for worldly wealth increased very fast; but he had no faith in the honesty of any man, for he would part with nothing without ready money. His inclination to see others well employed, was greater than to work himself; and, as his wealth increased, his displeasure at its author increased also. The complaint was applicable to him that the prophet used concerning the Jews, ' When Ephraim waxed fat, he kicked.' "

It was observed that his wife and children became the chief object of his care; but this he concealed as much as possible—such conduct being contrary to the rules of the society. The women observed, too, that Mrs White paid more attention to her husband than to the rest of the society. " Although they sat at the same table with us," says Mr Innes, " they had tea in the evening. Mrs White said Friend Mother partook with them likewise, but no person ever saw her do that, and it was not believed by any one in the society; it was thought to be a cover only for the sugar, tea, and spirits, ordered by Mrs White."

George Hill, Mrs Muir, Mrs Gibson, and a few others, had been little accustomed to hard labour, and were still inclined to shift it off, which some of those who laboured hard began to notice and complain of to each other; for all knew they were acting in opposition to the will of Friend Mother, and they saw that she had enough to do to keep the working part of the society from quarrelling with the idlers.

A change was perceptible in Mr White's courtesy to Friend Mother. "I have heard him say to her, that the Irvine people had made her like the apostle Paul at Corinth—they esteemed her letters, but they said her personal appearance was not prepossessing, and that her manner of speaking was not only disagreeable, but was even contemptible. She was not permitted to go from home; and at length, under pretence of preserving the peace of the society, she was restricted from communicating to strangers who visited us, or even to members of the society, any thing he thought might endanger their peace. Even what he had himself published to the world, was not allowed to be mentioned. When she refused to be thus restricted by him, he became very boisterous, and would threaten either to leave her, or to disperse the society.

"Although Mr White was evidently more disappointed than any other person in the society, by the failure of the great event so ardently expected by him at the close of the fast, we all knew well he could not leave her of whose divine mission he had written and said so much. He had left neither property nor means behind to which he could return, and his character as a minister was lost. He could not labour with his hands to support himself and family, as others had done who had left the society, and he would have been ashamed to beg. But even had he attempted to have done so, I think he would not have obtained a morsel of meat or a night's quarters in any part of Great Britain where he was known. Therefore, like John, he remained fretting under his disappointment.

"I had good reason to know that Mr White and his wife used frequently to accuse our Friend Mother, in private, of being a deceiver, for not obtaining for them that personal translation, in the hopes of which they had left their all, and had followed her through all the troubles and persecutions both at Irvine and Closeburn. Friend Mother sometimes told the women who were friendly with her how she was treated, but she did so always with a caution not to interfere with them on her account, as it would only tend to make things worse; for they now despised her counsel, and had become so hardened under reproof, that she was thenceforth resolved to allow them to take correction from the effects of their own deeds." Her mind was certainly in a very disturbed state, when she wrote the letter from which the following is an extract, to her friend Mrs Muir, who was then absent on a visit:—

(No date.)

"Oh hasten, my dear, to return to us, and leave the dead weights of this world, who have ever been using all their strength to break the branches of the trees that have been planted by the Lord. . . . Although the world's warfare and mine will soon be at an end here, their judgment is not lingering, nor their damnation slumbering. I sorrow because they will not cease from sin. Woe to the adulterers and adulteresses that have been with me! They have gone on in the way of Cain, and run greedily after the error of Balaam for reward, and, by all appearance, will perish in the gainsaying of Cor. Yet they will not let Mercy prevent their eternal misery; they are so bent on the pleasures of sin, because they fear they are but to last a short time; the devil rages now in the breasts of the children of disobedience, as a wild bull in a net; but the days of our mourning shall be ended, and eternal joy shall be on our heads. . . . They have scorned Mercy in the height of their pride, for no other reason than the showing them love in the depth of their humility. It has not been in ignorance they have acted so, for it has always been the case, because judgment was not speedily executed. This from your mother in the Lord, ELSPATH SIMPSON."

Andrew Innes is of opinion that this letter refers

to the fast, and how the judgment then expected was delayed by the prolongation of mercy, which strengthened, even at Auchengibbert, her enemies against her ; but he wholly overlooks the reference made by her to the character of the persons by whom she was surrounded, which appears to be a departure from the tenets on her part, which permitted a community of women, and held that they could commit no moral sin. If any doubt existed as to the illicit intercourse of the sexes, it is dissipated by the admission here made by the founder of the sect herself. The reader may form some idea of the nature of the crimes, of which a concealment could have been maintained from the public for so many years.[1]

"After Friend Mother was debarred from leaving the house, she generally sat beside the women at their spinning-wheels, and only whispered to them at times, for her spirit was evidently broken. She was plainly seen to be in a declining state of health, but few were willing to observe it. One day, she said before us all—'Since I cannot prevent some of you going hell-ward, I will cast my body down in your way, and those who wish to do so, may go over it.' One of the women said, she was grieved to hear her speak in that strain ; to which she replied, 'I go where my words will not be rejected.' As we

---

[1] Mr Ross, the present proprietor of Auchengibbert, informed me lately, that bones are yet turned up occasionally by the plough on a certain part of that farm, supposed to be remains of the Buchanite children which had been interred there

thought these words applied to Mr White and a few others, at whose conduct she was grieved, we paid little attention to them at the time, as no one thought she would die. But on the morning of the 29th March 1791, as the ploughman was engaged in the fields, and I employed in the barn, one of the women came running from the house to inform us that Friend Mother was exceedingly ill. I made all the haste I possibly could to the house, but never supposed her to be in a dying state, till I entered the closet where she lay. The bed was surrounded by both men and women, who seemed all greatly agitated, with the exception of Mrs White. Mr White urged them to be quiet, and to keep further from the bed; but I pressed forward, and was just in time to see her draw her last breath. Nothing was then to be seen, but the deepest emotions of distress—nothing heard but the unsubdued wailings of heartfelt sorrow."

Just before Mother Buchan had become speechless, she exhorted the bystanders to continue steadfast and unanimous in their adherence to the doctrines which she had taught them. She said they had received a convincing proof that she was the Spirit of God, that Christ was her elder brother, and that she was consequently the third person in the Godhead, or, in other words, the Holy Ghost, and therefore could not die. And although she should appear to do so, they need not be discouraged, for she would only sleep; and if their faith was pure without alloy, she, at the end of six days, would return for them. But if they still remained faithless, she would not return to take them to heaven till the end of ten years, when, if they still continued unprepared for that change, fifty years would elapse before she would reappear on earth; but she would then, at all events, descend to convince the faithless world of its error, in supposing her to be only one of the false prophets mentioned in the eighteenth chapter of Deuteronomy, and that her reappearance in the world would be a certain prelude to the fulfilment of the threatened judgment of the Lord.

"Mr White having invited two gentlemen from Dumfries to call at Auchengibbert that day, on their way home from Kirkpatrick-Durham fair, was very anxious to get the corpse out of the way before their arrival, that they might not learn what had happened. There being plenty of boards at hand, a coffin was made with all possible dispatch, but without planing or blacking. I was so depressed that I could not assist in making it, but I helped to lay her in it. Every one was overwhelmed with grief while we were thus employed. And what was most singular, our hands, after touching her, emitted an odoriferous perfume, as if we had been handling myrrh or some other aromatic herb, which spread over the room.

"As soon as the coffining was over, she was carried privately to the barn for concealment; and as the lid of the coffin was not permitted to be nailed down, she was frequently visited by every member of the society. One morning, some of the women, who went, as usual, to visit her, came running back suddenly, with the news that she had really risen from the dead, which instantly raised an awful commotion. The fear of guilt in having placed her in a coffin, with the intention of burying her, struck them all with such terror, that none had courage to approach the barn to ascertain if the body was really gone. I happened at that time to be working at a short distance from the house, but on hearing the weeping and wailing, my attention was turned towards it. Mr White was standing in front of the house, wringing his hands, seemingly in a state of distraction; his wife was tearing the hair out of her head in handfuls; George Hill was surrounded by several of the women, all weeping bitterly.

"Upon learning the cause of this unaccountable scene of distress, I instantly ran to the barn along with George Kidd, and upon ascertaining that the corpse was lying on the very place where it was at first laid, I dispatched George to inform Mr White that the alarm which had given them so much trouble, was false. This intelligence had the effect of turning their sorrow and fear into joy; but this sensation was only momentary, as the women who had raised the alarm, insisted that the coffin was empty when they examined it. I was immediately accused by one and all of them, of having concealed the body in order to deceive them; and I might just as well have attempted to drive back the flowing tide, as to have persuaded them to the contrary. What made the matter worse for me was, some people having visited Duncan Robertson, the wheelwright, in the way of business, on observing the sad commotion our people were in, enquired the cause; upon which Duncan told them the reason, before the error was discovered. This made them exclaim more vehemently against me, being, as they said, the cause of bringing them to shame."

A platform had been erected in the centre of the barn, on which the coffin, containing the body, was placed; but the lid of the coffin was not nailed down, in order that no obstruction might be placed in the way of her ascension! As the first period for her return drew near a close, those who were in the secret waited in breathless expectation for the commencement of her re-animation; but only a few of Mr White's disciples were permitted to enter the barn on the last evening of the *lake-wake,* if it might be so called. During the night, how they disposed of the body no one but themselves knew; but having cut a hole in the roof of the barn, exactly above where the corpse lay, they next day told the rest of Luckie's deluded followers that an angel had come and carried her away before their eyes, and, as a certain proof of the truth of this assertion, showed the aperture in the roof of the barn, through which they had ascended.

Mother Buchan had not a more zealous adherent than Andrew Innes; but, not enjoying the confidence of Mr White at the time of her death, he was not permitted to witness the removal of her

---

[1] Castle-Douglas Miscellany, vol. iii, No. 137.

body from the barn, to which circumstance he thus alludes:—" I went to bed at my usual time, and when I awoke early in the morning, was surprised to see James Sanders in the room, till he informed me he had been placed there to watch lest I should rise and disturb the people in the barn, a thing never meditated by me. I was aware that I was accounted an alien by Mr White and others of the society, from the time of my having returned from banishment, but the strongest proof I had of this being the case, was the attempt to deceive me as to the disposal of the remains of Friend Mother."

A more detailed description of the last illness and death of Luckie Buchan, will here find its proper place, as written by Andrew Innes at a subsequent period:—

"About this time an elder from the adjoining parish of Kirkpatrick-Durham came to get some work done by Duncan Robertson, who had been several times in Friend Mother's company during the short time we lived at Tarbreach. She brought him in to dine with us. After dinner, she said to him. as she knew he had sat often at the Lord's table as an elder of the established church, 'Can you tell me what makes this table differ from any other table?' He replied, the bread and wine dispensed at the communion table, were representatives of Christ's body and blood, which was not the case with bread and wine consumed at other tables. She then explained the difference between a symbolical and real union, during which Mr White sat silently listening, which was not his usual custom; but so soon as the elder was gone, he abused her for the liberty she had taken. Another time, when he had her in his own room, he was so loud with his abuse, and threatening to give up the farm and turn us all adrift, that Jean Gardner came into the parlour where we were all sitting, crying bitterly, and calling us to come fast, for Mr White was murdering Friend Mother, upon which we all rose and rushed to the door; but in my haste I came against an old woman, and caused her to fall in the passage, and another person following me in the dark, fell over her. Friend Mother hearing the noise, and being aware of the cause of it, came out, saying, the hurting of an innocent person was not the way to afford her relief.

" But I must now hasten to the object which you so anxiously wish to know—that is, the manner of her death. I am sure you will wonder much when I tell you, that notwithstanding so many warnings, her death came upon us very unexpectedly.

" One morning, not coming in to speak at breakfast as usual, we were all desired, after our morning meal was over, to go into Mr White's room. She was in bed, but spoke to us individually. Observing George Hill looking steadfastly at her, she said, ' Take a good look of me, George, that you may know me again; did you ever see a person in the jaws of death, with a countenance so composed as I have?' He made no reply. Even then there was not an individual of our society there, who could allow a single thought of her death to rest on the mind for a moment, with the exception of White and his wife. After this interview we left the room, and went all to our daily employment, but in about an hour and a half afterwards I heard a scream, and on looking out of the barn-door where I was at work, I saw Jean Gardner at the kitchen-door wringing her hands, and when she saw me she cried aloud, ' Oh, waes me, our Friend Mother is gone!' I instantly threw down the flail, and ran to where I had so shortly before seen her in life. They were all gathered round her; she breathed for a little time after I went in, but spoke no more.

"So soon as she had ceased to breathe, Mr White ordered us all out of the room, except those that were necessary to dress the corpse, for he had an appointment that day with a Mr Coultard, from Dumfries, in consequence of which the room behoved to be cleared; and he ordered my brother Joseph and I to get a coffin ready as fast as possible; but I refused, and Duncan Robertson supplied my place.

"He gave strict orders that no lamentation should be made, nor any appearance of her death seen amongst us, lest the account of her demise should get into the country, as we would then be annoyed with visitors; so every one was ordered to his usual employment. I returned to the barn, and watched there till I saw the two men carry into the house the hastily made coffin. I did not wait to be called into the house, but followed as fast as my feet could carry me. I saw the coffin opened at the bedside, and the body laid into it. One of the women complained of the simple dress bestowed upon the corpse, upon which Mr White replied, she always liked a plain simple dress best when alive; and he thought she was just laid out to her liking when dead.

"The savoury perfume that rose from her body, ere the lid of the coffin was laid down, filled the room with its fragrance. No one spoke, but all looked with seeming surprise, as well they might.

"The ceremony of the coffining being over, I returned to the barn, but after a time had elapsed, James Sanders, the man who had married Friend Mother's eldest daughter, came to me and said they could not agree about a burying-place for her—the women were against her being taken out of the house at all, but could not fix on a place to keep her in; they had, however, agreed to take her to an empty part of the barn that was used as a granary, so soon as it was dark. This plan pleased me well, as there was no partition between it and the other part of the barn, but only a mow of corn. When the time of removal came, I was as ready to assist as any of them. She was placed there, and the door locked, but I was not allowed to have the key; but that gave me little trouble, as I always kept the key of the door of the other part of the barn, and could easily reach the place where she was laid, by climbing over the corn-mow; so they carried the key with them, and considered all safe until a burying-place should be fixed upon afterwards.

"Next morning, when the women came into the granary to see the corpse, I listened and heard them say that they would never consent to her being buried outside the house, for when they used to say to her, that they were afraid the bad usage she was receiving at the hands of Mr White would at length provoke the Lord, so that he would come and take her away from them, she always replied there was no fear of that, for if she was not put away, she would not be taken away; but she thought he might allow her corpse to remain as long unburied, as Jesus lay in the tomb of Joseph. When I heard them agree that there was no occasion for their returning to the barn that day, it immediately started into my mind that I had it now in my power to prevent her being buried, at least for some time, by concealing her among the sheaf corn; it, however, occurred to me that if I took away the coffin, I would be immediately suspected as having only played off some trick on them. I therefore prepared a place for her among the corn, and removed the body only into it, and covered it up again, without consulting or letting it be known to any person what I had done. But I could not sleep one wink that night. I knew that swarms of rats infested the barn, and I was afraid lest some of them might push through the sheaf corn and get to the corpse. I therefore rose by peep of day, and went direct to the barn, but I was not in many minutes, till I heard the lock of the granary door opened and some of our women walk in, and presently heard a person exclaim, 'Oh, the coffin is empty, Friend Mother is gone! What will become of us now?' Then they all began to accuse themselves for allowing Mr White to send her out of the house, and off they went to inform their companions of what had taken place, after which, one and all of the inmates of the house fell upon Mr White, for having killed Friend Mother by his avarice and love of worldly man's approbation, while he sat as a condemned criminal before his accusers, but made no defence.

"I am writing here by report, as I did not leave the barn, and I cannot recollect of being among them at breakfast, but I recollect distinctly of the women bringing in some strangers into the granary that came on business to the wheelwright, and heard them all exclaiming as to the empty coffin, which I was sorry to hear, but could not prevent; so I continued at my work notwithstanding their restless position.

"On looking out of the barn-door, I observed Mr White with a woman on each side supporting him, while he attempted to walk in a field adjoining the house, at which time George Hill came into the barn, and said he wondered how I could work, and all the rest of the society in such a sad condition. He thought I certainly knew something of her that none of the rest did, otherwise I could not be so seemingly careless of what gave them all so much concern. He desired me just to look at Mr White, and I would easily perceive what agony he was in. I could not think of keeping them longer in such distress, and therefore told him plainly where I had concealed her, and said he was at liberty to make this public in the society. I continued to work until I heard them take her out of the corn, and replace her in the coffin, all the while abusing me with as much bitterness as they had previously done Mr White; and I then slipped away to my bed, and lay down, clothes and all, until it was dark, when James Sanders came in and sat down at my bedside. He said they were just going to bury her, and that he had been sent to watch me, lest I should get up and again disturb them; so I remained quietly in bed till all was over."

Had the removal of the earthly remains of Luckie Buchan from the barn, been the trick of a frolicsome scapegrace, the reader might then have concluded, that a wish to hear the exclamations of the astonished Buchanites, when it was discovered that the coffin in the barn was empty and the corpse gone, and the search that was likely to ensue, was the cause of his doing so. Or had it been the doing of an unbeliever of the society, who, seeing that the death of the old woman had laid bare the fallacy of her pretensions to a divine mission, and, by producing the corpse afterwards, to convince his associates that she had not ascended to heaven as anticipated, a measure that would soon overturn the society; then, there might have appeared some method in this mad trick of the incomprehensible Andrew. But it is now manifest, that it was the superstitious act of her first and still most ardent adherent, performed, as will ultimately appear, in the assurance that such a pious demonstration of unerring faith would ensure his personal translation to heaven, without " entering the dark shade of the valley of death."

The daughters of Mrs Buchan, formerly mentioned, became members of the society when at Irvine, and remained with it till about two years before their mother's death, when they left it on account of the treatment she received from Mr White. The elder, named Margaret, formed an alliance with James Sanders, who joined the society at Closeburn, and was a native of that neighbourhood; but she left him in the society, and went to Thornhill. Ann went to Glasgow to her father, and married there a sailor named Goldie; who having been drowned, she soon after returned to Thornhill, and was assisting her sister in keeping a small school at the time of her mother's death. So annoyed were they by the reports that reached them hourly of that event, that, acting under the advice of their friends, they came to Galloway, and presented a petition to Sir Alexander Gordon of Greenlaw, then stewart-depute of the stewartry of Kirkcudbright, to cause Mr White to produce the remains of their mother, for the purpose of allaying the public clamour, as well as enabling them to discharge the last filial duties to their deceased parent. On being served with a copy of this petition, Mr White addressed the stewart-depute as follows:—

"Mains of Auchengibbert, 19th April 1791

" HONOURABLE SIR,

"This day I have been served with the copy of a petition which has been presented to your honour, at the instance of Margaret and Ann Buchan; in which petition they complain that their mother had not been interred, that they had come to me to inquire into the matter, and had got no satisfaction; and, finally, they importuned your lordship to compel me to produce the body.

"Be it known to your honour, that there is not one word of truth in the whole petition. I never saw either Margaret or Ann Buchan at Auchengibbert inquiring about the above matter; and however much they may say in their petition concerning their duty and affection towards their mother, true it is, they acted a very inimical part towards her when in life: they often vented language unbecoming children of common discretion, and often said they wished their mother's head was under the ground. This I mention to your lordship, to show you the character of these now pretended dutiful petitioners. They never came near their mother in her last illness—no, nor for two years before, although often in the neighbourhood.

" But for your honour's further information—consequently after their mother was six days dead, I caused her to be interred in the way my prudence thought best. There was such a clamour about that person in the country when in life, that a public interment after the common manner, would have raised a mob—a noise, and speeches inconsistent with sobriety and Christianity, which disorder I know your lordship hates.

" Their seeking the body at this time to inter, is

truly improper. It has been dead full three weeks already, and another interment after so long a time, would be a measure truly dangerous to the country. Baneful plagues have been occasioned by a less cause; and I am sure your lordship, whose office and disposition are engaged to protect the country from such dangers, (which rash persons might cause,) would highly discourage such a procedure.

"And as I never heard of a law in this country obliging one to bury in a public manner, or in any place more than another, excepting in cases of suicide, consequently I am not conscious of having broken any law in the part I have acted in the above matter. I thought it most proper to transmit this intelligence to your honour, hoping that it will answer the end better than lodging answers with the clerk of court. But if your lordship still thinks it better to answer their petition in a formal legal way, may I beg that you will signify so by the bearer, and every thing, as far and as soon as possible, shall be done to satisfy your lordship.—With much respect, I remain, honourable sir, your most humble servant, (Signed) HUGH WHITE."

The public agitation was so great on this subject, that Sir Alexander Gordon did not deem it prudent to endanger the public peace by making the disinterment of Mrs Buchan the subject of public investigation; but he caused Mr White to meet him at midnight, at a place named for that purpose, in the neighbourhood of Auchengibbert; and that he found the remains of Mrs Buchan, will be shown in due time. Some people asserted, that she was buried under the hearth-stone of the kitchen of the farm-house at Auchengibbert; others affirmed, that she was sunk in Auchengibbert loch; but so well was the secret kept as to the real place of interment, that upwards of thirty years afterwards, her daughter, Mrs Goldie, believing the remains of her mother to be still kept in the house occupied by the Buchanites at Crocketford, caused the following search to be made by a grandson of Mrs Buchan, which I give in the words of Andrew Innes, from the MS. in my possession:—"I intended to have finished Mrs Goldie's history here, but I must not omit giving you a sketch of a visit made to us by her nephew. I cannot state the very time, but he appeared one day at the gate very unexpectedly. On seeing him, the women were all alarmed, as they thought he was come to put us all out of the house by some quirk of law. I went and put his horse into the stable; he then told me he had come to search the house, for his aunt had told him she had reasons to fear her mother's remains had never been buried, but were concealed in some part of the house; and that he was resolved to ascertain if that was really the case. I said, he might soon satisfy himself in that respect, as I would go with him direct to the suspected place; on which he replied, that it was a little closet at the top of the stair. As the closet has no window, I went into the kitchen and brought a lighted candle, with which I showed him the place, where was a large old chest, in which, I suppose, he expected to find the remains of his grandmother, as he raised the lid, and lifted out all the blankets and spare bed-clothes it contained, of which it was nearly full, without finding what he was in search of. He then took the candle in his own hand and went up to the garret, but soon returned, saying there was no such thing there. I then urged him to search other parts of the house, but he declined doing so, saying he was now satisfied that he had been deceived."

"Considering that Mrs Buchan was an illiterate woman, and the wife of a potter, without any influence arising from rank, and that she took the dangerous step of deserting her husband, associating with a promiscuous company, and regulating their affairs, she met with surprising success. She must have been a person of very quick parts, and, amid all her ravings, of much practical knowledge of human nature. She could strike the passions that lie deep in the human bosom. Like Mahomet, she never ventured upon working miracles, which afford a palpable way of detecting an impostor; but insisted on implicit faith. . . 'James, John, Andrew, and Peter,' said she, 'sought no sign to leave their nets. Matthew sought none to leave the receipt of customs. They loved Jesus and the *call* he gave them; and they needed salvation, which was sign enough for them.' So she wrote in 1786: but in a few years 'she descended to the grave;' and then where was her sign? It served her during her lifetime, but it failed at her death. The sheriff, with his warrant, closed the grave over all her pretensions."[1]

"On this occasion, according to common report, Mr White acted very disingenuously: he pretended at first she was only in a trance; and when that pretence could not avail any longer, he had her buried clandestinely, without the knowledge of her votaries, alleging, as is said, that she was taken up to heaven. A magistrate, however, taking the business in hand, he was obliged, to his great mortification and confusion, to produce the body."[2]

The reader is already aware of Mrs Buchan's last words, namely, that she would undoubtedly return to the world again at the end of fifty years from that time. Meanwhile, we will proceed with an account of the transactions of her followers up to that period.[3]

---

[1] Struthers' History of the Relief Church. Glasgow, 1843, pp 345, 346

[2] Christian Journal for January 1835, p. 12.

[3] Soon after the death of Mrs Buchan, but before the account of it had reached the town of Irvine, Mr Hunter, who left the society at the fast, met there a horse-dealer, who had just returned from Dumfries fair :—" What news from the south country, John?" inquired the little hump-backed old man "None that I remember," replied the dealer, "except that your old friend Luckie Buchan is dead at last." "Oh no, John," rejoined Mr Hunter; ' that is not the case, and never will be in this world!" "Well," said John, hastily, "if she is not dead, her friends in Galloway have played her a devilish trick, for they have buried her "—Letter from M Montgomery, Irvine, 16th Feb 1836

CHAPTER V.

Mr White publicly recants all he has advanced respecting the divine mission of Mrs Buchan—Those of the society who entertain a similar opinion, proceed with him to America—Account of them in the New World—Jean Gardner the person referred to by Burns in his epistle to David Sillar—The true Buchanites remove to Larghill, a wild moorland farm—They continue to hold the "faith and practice" inculcated by their founder—They subsequently remove to Crocketford, where, as they die, they are buried in the kail-yard—Anecdotes of some of the members who died there—The Buchanite dwelling-house at Crocketford described—Peculiarities of its inmates at the time my correspondence commenced with Andrew Innes, the last of the sect—Multiplicity and bent of his writings—His fanciful intercourse with the shade of Mrs Buchan, as my errand-boy—His extraordinary conduct on hearing that I had discovered the first temporary burial-place of Mrs Buchan—The time of the expected advent of Mrs Buchan passes without altering his faith—His death, and interment with the remains of Mrs Buchan

THE pecuniary circumstances of the Buchanites appear to have been in a flourishing state at the time of Mrs Buchan's death, as compared with their entry to the farm of Auchengibbert. The rent was paid till the following term of Whitsunday; there were thirteen stacks of corn in the barn-yard, seven horses in a newly-built stable, seven milch cows in the byre, and a large stock of black cattle on the hill, with a stock of sheep and swine. The people had two suits of clothes each, nearly new, with several webs of linen and woollen cloth in store. Such was the progress made by industry in a high-rented farm, in the course of a few years. But I must now return to the words of my narrator.

"I noticed formerly, that Mr White's situation with our Friend Mother, was in many respects like that of John the Baptist with Jesus Christ. When Mr White left Irvine, he was as desolate as John the Baptist when he took up the cross; and he exercised his office, as chief of an apostolic dispensation, in nearly the same manner as John did. The latter lost his life, by taking a wrong step in the execution of his office; Mr White erred, in not doing what he advised others to do. He affirmed in his publications, both in prose and verse, that the author of our society was the very person foreseen by St John, as mentioned in the Revelation. While at Closeburn, he always assisted her in explaining to us her particular views of Scripture; but it was not so at Auchengibbert. When, after meals, she addressed herself to different persons, before the fast he always assisted her, but after that period he sat and listened like others, but never assisted as he had previously done.

"The failure of personal translation at the fast, destroyed all hope of reward for his sufferings, and this was what prevented him from receiving the benefit of her words and actions like others; and the confidence that many had in him, on seeing this change, had a great effect on them also.

"After the departure of our Friend Mother, when he had got all things, as he thought, settled to his mind, he began to boast over us for our ignorance in not seeing what she really was,—telling us he had long seen her in a declining state, and would have informed us of her mortality, if we had not been so determinedly ignorant and bigoted, that he durst not presume to mention it to us; and that he did not now believe that she was the divine person he had represented her to be in his writings, but he believed that, like Moses, she had done all that was intended for her to do in the world, and had left him, like Joshua, to finish the work; and, if we would accept of him in that capacity, we would find him faithful and diligent for our interest. Two-thirds of the people immediately agreed to his proposal,—some through fear, and others who had left Irvine and joined the society on his account, continued friendly to him. But Duncan Robertson, George Kidd, and myself, dissented publicly, as did Christian Robertson, on which account she had a very disagreeable life afterwards, as she still contended it was the bad usage Friend Mother received from Mr and Mrs White, that was the cause of her death; and she brought things to light which Mr White did not suppose were known to any of us. He was very much enraged against her, so that she was obliged to leave the room where the women sat at their wheels, and go to some other place with her work for a time; but, as she was one of the best spinners in the society, Mr White was afraid of losing her, and that modified his manners towards her.

" The other man and myself who refused to submit to his government, had seen enough of his selfishness previously, but we followed our work as formerly—either in the fields or in the out-houses, and were, consequently, not often with him. He continued for some time to sit at table with us, and to exhort us in the manner our Friend Mother was wont to do; but his doctrine became so offensive, and opposite to what we had formerly heard and believed, that we grew quite careless of hearing him, and often rose from table, under some pretence, without waiting till his discourse was finished, which sometimes gave him great offence. His attendance at our table gradually grew less frequent, and, consequently, his exhortations also. I, for one, was not sorry on that account.

"At length he threw off all pretensions of being separated from his wife and children, and began to get the latter educated fit for worldly employment. He encouraged others to marry, and at last publicly condemned all he had written and published. The great wonders seen and enjoyed at the fast, were all soon buried out of sight by selfishness. I was astonished to see how her words and actions, even at Auchengibbert, were passed by and forgotten by her most intimate friends, so that I am not surprised at her words and actions being misrepresented by those who never saw her.

"Mr White always endeavoured to persuade us, that without his skill and good management, we could not support ourselves, and yet he was lightly esteemed by many of us, notwithstanding the benefit we were receiving by him. He often said he would find a way to make us sensible of what he was doing for us, but we paid little attention to these threatenings for about a year,—working faithfully all the time, and allowing him to reap the profit; till one day he became so exceedingly enraged against George Kidd the ploughman, on account of some trifling affair, that when we were all assembled at meal-time, he came into the room, and declared that he was determined to make us all obey him, and since he could not obtain submission by serving us, he would make us obey by compulsion. As none of our names whom he considered refractory, were in the lease of the farm, he said he would swear the peace against us, and thereby compel us to find bail for our future good behaviour, or else go to prison; or, failing that, he would send us all adrift.

"Matters were now come to such a height, that we had little doubt of his putting either of these threats in force. After dinner, therefore, a few of us met privately, and agreed that I should take a lease of a neighbouring farm of 400 acres. Finding the proprietor willing to let it on what we considered reasonable terms,[1] Duncan Robertson, George Kidd, and myself, took it jointly for several years. We very soon informed Mr White of what we had done, but said we would continue to work at Auchengibbert, and would keep Larghill[2] (our

[1] The rent was sixteen pounds the first year, and twenty guineas per annum afterwards, which was little more than one shilling an acre.

[2] It may be here mentioned, that the farm of Larghill, part of the estate of Larglanglee, formerly belonged to the celebrated Laird of Lag, who bore such a conspicuous part in the time of the Persecution in Galloway and Ayrshire —Ancient and Modern Valuation Roll of the Stewartry of Kirkcudbright, pp. 104, 107, edit. 1820.

new farm) as a led farm, if we only got peace to do so; but he rejected our offer with scorn, saying, he would go to America, as he knew that country well; nor could he afterwards be dissuaded from the resolution he had thus taken, and all the people of his party resolved to accompany him — they would amount in all to about thirty. Lest Mr Bushby, the proprietor of the land which we occupied, might prevent them from transferring their lease of it to another person, Mr White and George Hill applied to a person who purchased the greater part of the stock and growing crop; no opposition being offered by those persons in the society who still believed in the divine mission of our Friend Mother, and who wished to remain near the spot of her departure."

Being fully prepared for the journey, they moved away in a body from Auchengibbert for America, early in the morning of the 11th June 1792. They had two carts laden with clothes and provisions; the people, all on foot, took the road to Portpatrick. On arriving at Newry, finding a vessel ready to sail for Newcastle on the Delaware, they all embarked on board of her for that port.

From the recantation made by Mr White to the members of the society, so soon after the death of Mrs Buchan, there are no grounds to suppose that it could have been for the purpose of propagating his dreamy mysticisms in the new world, that he prevailed on so many persons to cast their bread on the waters with him. But, having been a professor of theology in an American college, and knowing, as he said, the country well, many were induced on that account to accompany him across the Atlantic, under the assurance of his using every exertion in his power to promote their interests.

From communications received by Andrew Innes from his brother Joseph, who had joined Mr White's standard, and from letters got by the relations and friends of some of the other emigrants who followed his fortunes, the following particulars have been obtained.

After a stormy passage of eight weeks, they landed at Newcastle on the Delaware, where Joseph Innes and a few others remained, whilst the rest advanced into the country. George Hill, in the first instance, took up his residence in Philadelphia, but afterwards proceeded to Baltimore. Mr White went to Virginia,—all providing for themselves in the best way they could. Of Mrs Muir, the friend and correspondent of Mrs Buchan, no satisfactory account ever reached this country; and, with the exception of Joseph Innes, who died in 1835, possessed of property worth upwards of £8000, all the others were peculiarly unfortunate.

George Hill, on arriving in Ireland, had married Jean Gardner, but she died of fever in Philadelphia, in 1793. It may be recollected, that our national bard, Robert Burns, in a letter to a friend in Montrose, dated August 1784, says, when he was working in Irvine as a flax-dresser, he was intimately acquainted with several persons who afterwards became zealous Buchanites. One of these was Miss

Jean Gardner just referred to. In his well-known epistle to David Sillar, Burns says—

> "You have your Meg, your dearest part,
> And I my darling Jean."

It has been hitherto generally supposed, that the female alluded to was Jean Armour, afterwards Mrs Burns, but I have every reason to believe that it was Jean Gardner. Andrew Innes says, " When I was sent back from Thornhill for Mr Hunter, Jean Gardner came with me from Irvine to Closeburn, and when we were in the neighbourhood of Tarbolton, she seemed to be in fear, and rather in a discomposed condition; when I inquired the cause, she said, it was lest Burns the poet should see her, for if he did, he would be sure to interrupt her, for they had long been on terms of intimacy; but we proceeded on our journey, without meeting with any obstruction."

Burns frequently visited her in the society, both at New Cample and at Auchengibbert. It is singular this heroine of Burns should have escaped the notice of all the biographers of the bard. She was certainly a young woman of very surpassing beauty, and is yet particularly remembered in the neighbourhood of Auchengibbert, for her personal attractions. Many persons recollect of having heard her name mentioned, on account of her beauty, who never saw her. George Hill, her husband, was employed for a short time as a clerk in a printing office in Philadelphia, and afterwards carried on business as a bookseller in Baltimore; but having, by the failure of a shipping company with which he was concerned, lost all he possessed, he was reduced to the most abject poverty. On learning his reverse of fortune, the few remaining Buchanites in this country offered to send him money to pay his passage home, if he wished to return, with the assurance of all the support they could render him in this country; but it was supposed he died of a broken heart, ere he could accept the friendly offer of his former associates.

Mrs White also died of fever about a year after her arrival in America, and left her husband with three children, one of whom was born only a few weeks before her death; Mr White was then a schoolmaster in a small village in the state of Virginia, and preached occasionally to a few Universalists, but never mentioned any of his former whimsical doctrines.

Before leaving this country, Mr White had evidently seen his folly in setting a time for the downpouring of the judgments mentioned in the revelation of St John, and thereby dooming the world to certain destruction, as well as denouncing all the sciences and college education in general as mere devices of the devil; as, a few weeks after his hopes were at the highest, he saw the failure of the vagaries of his imagination, and in a few years was under the necessity of betaking himself to his education, for the support of himself and family in a foreign land. He evidently threw away every advantage of nature and education, to become the leader of a new sect; and, on the failure of his denunciations, found himself a laughing-stock, or an object of commiseration, to the world at large.

The separation of the Buchanites, which took place on so many of their number emigrating to America, appears to have led to the mistake so often repeated since by various authors, that, on the death of their leader, which consequently put an end to their hopes of reaching the New Jerusalem without tasting death, they dispersed, and, consequently, the sect immediately became extinct.[1]— There was, however, a remnant left at the place of her demise. The number of these faithful believers in the divine mission of their founder, was only fourteen, among whom were three old women—two of whom came out of England: one, Susan Angus, was confined to bed for three years before her death; and the other, Dorothy Andrew, was blind; she lived in the society for twenty years—both of them, before joining, had been receiving parish aid; the third, Agnes Wylie, came from Irvine, and at that time was become very frail. Besides women, several others who were of Mr White's party, would gladly have accompanied him to America, had he permitted them to have done so; but he admitted only such as could defray their own expenses of the voyage, and, in all probability, could earn a livelihood in that quarter of the globe.

Immediately on the departure of Mr White and

---

[1] Buck's Theological Dictionary London 1827.

his followers, they removed from Auchengibbert to Larghill, in the parish of Urr—a dreary unenclosed waste, the sward of which had never been broken by an agricultural implement, and where a human dwelling had never been raised. By the division of stock at Auchengibbert, their allotment did not amount to £60, yet with that small sum did this singular sect commence a new struggle for subsistence. They took the sheep stock on the hill at a valuation, on credit; and the landlord having allowed them £5 to expend in the erection of houses, the women, as well as the men, assisted in building a cabin on the site of the ewe-buchts of the former tenant, which was almost the only green spot on the farm, in order to shelter them from the storm in the first instance. They afterwards enclosed a piece of moorland with a stone dyke for a garden. As they could not derive any support for a considerable time from the produce of this desolate tract, the women had recourse to their wheels, and Duncan Robertson to his handicraft of wheel-making.

The Buchanite women introduced into Galloway the two-handed spinning-wheel, in the use of which they were unrivalled in the south of Scotland: they frequently spun yarn to the fineness of seven dozen cuts to the pound, for the neighbouring gentry. Larghill soon became the emporium of industry. In that remote situation, they were visited by customers from many miles distant, as well as by persons beseeching medical aid, in the practice of which they were remarkably successful. Often, we are told, did the lancet of George Kidd, the diet drink or ointment prepared by Magdaline Gardner, remove distempers that had baffled the most skilful physicians. Mrs Alexander,[1] when a young woman, "remembers having accompanied a relative to Larghill, on a Sunday, to consult Magdaline Gardner as to the medical treatment of a young woman, who had taken the *falling sickness*,—when, to her utter astonishment, Sunday as it was, she saw several women seated at their wheels, spinning lint into yarn, a wheelwright working at his lathe, and a man thrashing corn in the barn." It is strange such a singular profanation of the Lord's Day should have been tolerated in the centre of a Christian community, in defiance of the rules of the Church of Scotland, and of the act of James VI., cap. 70.

The Buchanites were, however, obliging neighbours—for whatever kindness or favour they bestowed upon any person, it was always taken amiss if even thanks were returned for it. "No, no," said the donor, "she that has left us, gave us strict commands to do all the good we could : we are but fellow-mortals, and you must learn to give thanks to none but God, for to none else are thanks due." Such humane actions caused them to be now more respected, than they were formerly despised by their neighbours for their absurdities. They were all—males as well as females—dressed in clothes of their own manufacturing, of a light green colour. They

[1] Wife of William Alexander, cooper, Castle-Douglas.

were all of small stature, so that, had a stranger happened to meet any of them in their lonely farm, he would certainly have considered himself among the elfin race, rather than among mortals. All their farm utensils, barn and stable doors, barn fanners, corn-sacks, and carts, were marked in large characters with the words, "*Mercy's Property.*" Year after year, however, they became more assimilated to the people by whom they were surrounded. The tickets on their carts were changed to "The people of Larghill," and, latterly, to "George Kidd, farmer, Larghill;" but their fanners and sacks have the original mark to this day. This change in marking their carts, is thus explained in a letter which I received from Andrew Innes:—"We did not expect, at Larghill, a Mr White to rise again amongst us, but we found as much tyranny in George Kidd, as we did in him at Auchengibbert. As soon as the ground was fully stocked, houses built, and all debts paid, he informed us that we had nothing to expect from the stock; that we would be allowed the benefit of the crop, by paying one half of the rent; and though we expected other things, both Duncan Robertson and I submitted: he made wheels, I managed the crop, and wrought at my own trade when I could spare time to do so."

They adorned their garden with flowering shrubs, and planted fruit and forest-trees, thereby making Larghill really an oasis in the wilderness. Till the farm was fully stocked, and all debts paid off, every individual contributed freely, both labour and earnings, towards the general holding; but afterwards, by particular agreement, each man had his own department assigned to him, and the women performed their part of the farm work alternately,—occupying the rest of their time in spinning for their own use, or for payment, which they had at their disposal.

When the present military road between Dumfries and Castle-Douglas was first opened in the year 1800, the Buchanites purchased five acres of ground for houses and gardens at Crocketford, on one of which lots they built the first house of that village, which now contains upwards of 200 inhabitants. This house has since been occupied as the principal inn. At a more recent period, they built several others, so that the village of Crocketford is indebted to this remnant of the Buchanites for its origin, and might aptly enough have also been indebted to them for a name. In a recent communication, Mr Innes says, " Our purchase of land and building at Crocketford, has cost us upwards of £900.

The proprietor of Larghill, supposing the means thus expended in building to have been derived from the produce of his land possessed by the Buchanites, resolved to take it into his own management. They consequently removed, in 1808, to their premises at Crocketford, which was destined to be the Padanaram, or final resting-place, of the remaining members of the society. Their outward singularities having now disappeared, led many of their neighbours to suppose that their religious opinions had undergone a change also; but this does not appear to have been the case. They still continued to sing, after meat, what they called hymns, composed either by Andrew Innes or Duncan Robertson—for they, too, like Messrs White and Conyers, were aspirants for poetical honours. If a stranger were present at meal-time, they always sung the following doggerel rhyme—

> "The place shall be blessed where God's seed doth repose—
> By kindness to God's seed, no person shall lose—
> E'en a cup of cold water, that's handed in love
> To God's seed, will well be repaid from above"

It is stated by Andrew Innes, as a proof of the divinity of Mrs Buchan, that, during the eight years she remained with them, there was neither sickness nor death in the society, notwithstanding their having been cooped up together for such a length of time at New Cample, without almost any bedding or bed-clothes, and subsisting on a scanty supply of fare of the coarsest description. But it is to be recollected, the greater part of them were persons in the prime of life. The two old women who came from England, and Agnes Wylie from Irvine, died, and were secretly buried by permission of the laird, Mr Biggar, in the kailyard at Larghill. They were laid between the trees, and so close to the dyke, as to prevent their graves from being trodden on, or disturbed by the spade in digging the garden, when in possession of any future tenant. When the Buchanites formed their garden at Crocketford, they laid off a small plot of ground immediately behind the house, and sowed it with grass, seemingly for a small bleaching-green; but, on the death of one of their number, the survivors declared that this was to be their place of rest. Some of the neighbours wished to persuade them to take a burying-place in the parish churchyard, but their answer was, " No; we have kept ourselves separate from the rest of the world during our life, and our wish is to remain so when dead. The property is our own, and we have mutually agreed to have our dust deposited in that spot." A labourer was got to dig the grave, and a large company, male and female, was invited to attend; the corpse was interred in the usual form, and the whole company partook of a plentiful refreshment; but all the while none of those concerned showed any symptoms of grief, nor wore any of the usual badges of mourning. This has since continued to be the place of their interment, and there are at length twelve of them laid there. The small piece of ground has lately been enclosed by a stone-and-lime wall, of about three feet in height.

Mrs Gibson, known only in the society by her maiden name of Magdaline Gardner, was the first who died at Crocketford, and was buried in the little spot just described. She was one of the first, and continued to be one of the most zealous adherents of Mrs Buchan. It was she who accompanied Mrs Buchan from Glasgow to Kirkintulloch in August 1783, when Andrew Innes was returning to Muthill. In October of the same year, as the reader may remember, after Mrs Buchan had been abused by the people of Irvine, she accompanied her to

Glasgow, and attended her there for many weeks, till she had recovered from the injury she had received, and supported her during the time. "When her husband left the society at Closeburn, he used every means in his power, as already stated, to persuade her to leave it also, but could not prevail on her to return with him to Irvine, though they were possessed of both houses and land, and were not encumbered with any family. When her husband heard of her death, he came to Crocketford to ascertain the truth of the report; and when he saw her grave, he belaboured it with his staff as if he had been correcting an unruly animal, and afterwards kicked it with his feet, using all the while the most coarse and abusive language towards her."

Jean Watt, also a native of Irvine, died in 1824, and was laid beside her old acquaintance, Magdaline Gardner. After her decease, two of her relations came to Crocketford, to claim what money she had left; but when they found they could not do so by law, they accepted £10 in lieu of all demands, and departed apparently well satisfied.

When George Kidd was on his death-bed, he was professionally attended by my friend Dr Howatson of Kirkpatrick. One evening, whilst visiting his patient, who was apparently on the very brink of the grave, the doctor, before leaving the house, was requested by Andrew Innes to say how long he thought his patient could live. "I think he will hardly see the morning," was the reply. Andrew was seemingly satisfied with the answer; but shortly after sunrise, next morning, a person arrived at the doctor's house, to request he would furnish his bill for attending George Kidd, who, not having died within the time specified by the doctor, his professional services were dispensed with, nor was he ever afterwards employed.

Duncan Robertson, though of humble pretensions, was a prominent person in the society from its commencement, and was one of the most stanch believers in the divine mission of Mrs Buchan. Just before his death, however, which happened on the 19th of January 1826, he wished to see a minister of the church, but this request was sternly rejected by the then four remaining members of the society. "Would you," said Andrew Innes, "make a fool of yourself at last, and of us also? No, Duncan; that will not do; ye must die as ye have lived—there shall no minister enter this house while I am alive."

Two years after the death of Duncan Robertson, I came to reside at Castle-Douglas, and had occasion to visit Crocketford, professionally, about once a month; but it was a considerable time after this before I became acquainted with Andrew Innes. Of the fourteen persons who took up their residence at Larghill, only Andrew, and Katherine Gardner, his reputed wife, were then alive. Although these two octogenarians had lived together for nearly sixty years, their domestic habits were of the most singular description. Katherine is thus alluded to by Andrew in his narrative:—

"Women are, and always have been, Satan's chief

instruments for ensnaring man. If a child is begotten, then Satan has the laws of the land in his power, and the woman is as willing to rise against the man, as the devil is. I am a witness of this, and also a sufferer; therefore I speak from experience. When our whole property was divided by those who went to America, the proportion to each amounted to only L.5, 9s. 11d., which we, who remained, had to accept in such articles, at a valuation, as could not be disposed of at the time. Some of the women, who were afraid of losing their proportion in the new farm of Larghill, required a little bill for the amount, to enable them to force payment when they might think fit to do so. Katherine Gardner was one of the number, nor were we long in Larghill till she required her money, and received it. She then left us, and rented a room to herself at Auchengibbert, but allowed her child, then five years old, to remain with us. Her motive for thus separating herself from the society, was to force me, either by by law to do the same, or to give her a separate maintenance. In this she followed the example of Mrs Sanders, Friend Mother's eldest daughter, who, after she left us at Auchengibbert, raised an action against her husband, who remained still with the society, for the support of herself and child.

" On finding she could not substantiate her claim against me, Katherine returned to Larghill, where she spun fine yarn for the people in the neighbourhood, always keeping the money which she received for work at her own disposal.

"We began to build our present house, two years before the expiry of our lease at Larghill, as we knew we would have then to remove. As soon as the house was habitable, Katherine removed to it, and still occupies the same room and closet which she then took possession of. She continued to work as usual, but did not appear at our table. She carried what she wanted of our provisions to her own room, cooked or otherwise, as she thought proper; and what she wanted for herself which we did not use, she purchased with her own money; and now that the other women are all dead, she lives very quiet and retired. She has been, I believe, considered by our neighbours as one of our society, though as much removed from the natural habits of that body as if she had lived in France; and I really think she could not relate distinctly a circumstance that happened in the society, except such as personally concerned herself.

"The form of marriage-contract, by which man and woman are united, should be, that they live together as long as they can agree—but if they cannot agree, then to separate—and I think the apostle Paul gives the same advice to the Corinthians. There is no necessity for the interference of the clergy; marriage is only a civil contract by the law of Scotland, and might it not be the same elsewhere?"

Such are the views of Andrew Innes respecting marriage; a proof that he followed up, to a certain extent, the views of Mrs Buchan, as expressed in her letter to Mr Brown of Sunderland.

The house occupied by Andrew Innes and his wife, though built in the present century, might be mistaken for one of the oldest dwelling-houses in Galloway. The storeys are low, the windows small, with clumsy sashes; and there being no mark of a chisel on any part of the building, an antiquary might easily be led to suppose the structure to have been erected prior to the introduction of such implements into this quarter. Such a supposition might be strengthened by the *onstead* falling into ruins. The little paved court in front of the house, is disfigured by water lodging where stones have been displaced; while goose-grass grows rank round the posts of the entrance-gate, several of the bars of which have been broken for many years. The disorderly state of the slates on the roof of the house, raise an apprehension that they are about to descend on the head of the first person who approaches the dwelling, and the neglected state of the once whitewashed walls, tends to give the habitation a desolate and comfortless appearance. Nor is the interior calculated to relieve the impression. The feeble light admitted by the small dusty windows, is just sufficient to show that the scanty furniture is of the coarsest description, and that the spider may take up his residence in any part of the house, without the least danger of being disturbed.

The antiquated appearance of the inmates is quite in accordance with the house and furniture. Old Katie, when seen in the twilight, with a broom in her hand, moving about the premises, or sauntering round the graves of the dead, might easily be supposed to be one of those ancient females, yet lingering in the world, whom we are told nightly rode on a broomstick through the air, and who could at pleasure reduce the size of their persons to that of a hare or a cat. Her stature, which, even in the prime of life, has evidently been diminutive, is now shrivelled, and so bent under the pressure of four-score years, that her height does not exceed fifty inches! Her head is increased to at least three times its natural size, by an incredible succession of caps and bandages, bound so closely over the upper part of her little hatchet face, as to meet a pair of black-horn mounted spectacles, which she generally wears, the bridge of which is wrapped round with coloured yarn, apparently to save the skin of her nose. Her neck, as if unable to support the enormous quantity of cloth by which it is overtopped, bends forward till her chin rests on her breast; thereby compressing, or as the head moves to either side, contorting the features of her little countenance, now the reverse of comely, into very disagreeable-looking forms. A loose camlet gown of a dark blue colour, reaching from her neck to her heels, completes all that is seen of her dress. Notwithstanding her extreme old age and seemingly delicate frame, old Katie is astonishingly active. The villagers say, she may be generally seen, like a Banshee, moving about the premises *in the gray of the morning,* tending the cows, or, when the corn is in the ear, scaring away the small birds from it, by the rattling of her iron-shod clogs on the stones.

She spends the latter part of the day at her wheel, either by the kitchen-fire, or in a small closet by herself; whilst another small apartment in the opposite end, is occupied by her husband, for whom she seems to have a tender regard.

Andrew being entitled, by the Reform Act, to vote for a member of parliament for the stewartry of Kircudbright, was about to be hurried away by some of his neighbours, to support Murray of Broughton at the general election of 1841; but although Castle Douglas, the polling-station, was only nine miles distant, Katie stoutly opposed his departure, for fear of his sustaining any bodily harm. Finding every remonstrance she could make not likely to detain him, she clung to his clothes and held him fast, till Grizzy, a faithful servant, who had been fifteen years in their service, volunteered to accompany him, for the purpose of bringing him safely back. As soon as Andrew alighted from the chaise which had been sent to convey him to the polling-booth, he dispatched his servant to inform me of his arrival. Though the crowd was great, by the kindness of some friends, I soon got him passed through the polling-place, and set at liberty. He took no interest whatever in the passing scene; and although I succeeded in amusing him for a short time at my house, he soon became as anxious to return to old Katie, as she had been to prevent his departure. Never having seen him recognise her, even although he met her in the passage of the house, and understanding that each, at all times, occupied a separate apartment, as before stated, and sat at different boards, I was surprised to hear him frequently say, " I wish I was home once more, as my poor Katie will be in a sad way, till I am safely seated again at my own fireside."

This simple incident shows, that neither old age, nor infirmities, nor the peculiarity of their domestic habits, had wholly extinguished the mutual attachment of these frail octogenarians.

Andrew Innes is in stature not more than five feet two inches high, and of rather a slender make; his thin gray hairs hang down below an old slouched hat, which seems permanently affixed to his head, as he wears it in-doors as well as out; from under this misshapen covering, appear his long shaggy eyebrows, overshadowing his little gray eyes, set far back in their sockets, and which, even at his advanced age, appear to retain much of their former expression. The general lineaments of his countenance strongly indicate traits of character, which, had they been properly directed in early life, might have made him a distinguished citizen, instead of a wild and enthusiastic bigot.

Since the green uniform of the Buchanite corps was laid aside, Andrew has generally worn a light drab-coloured short coat, vest and breeches of strong home-made cloth, rig-and-fur hose, and sky-blue spatterdashes, with bright buttons. When he goes abroad, he wears a moorland plaid-cloak, seemingly very old, as the collar is a good deal decayed, apparently, however, more from smoke than from the rays of the sun.

As he is not required, by his religious principles or business, to attend either church or market, he goes no further from home than to the village smithy or joiner's shop, to learn the local news of the day, or to receive a local newspaper, which he has joined for many years, at the rate of eightpence a quarter. This might be considered an instance of backsliding, as, during Mrs Buchan's lifetime, a newspaper was never seen in the hands of any member of the society, nor was any attention paid to passing events, whether local or general.

Although Andrew Innes has never studied the rules of prose composition, he writes with surprising facility. I have in my possession at present, several MSS. entitled, "Observations on Original Sin," "Observations on the Faith of Assurance," "Observations on a sermon for Young Women," and "Observations on Saving Grace." But these are not a tithe of his writings, on subjects tending to propagate the singular principles professed by Mrs Buchan, which appear to have been written with a view to convert some of his neighbours. He lends these MSS. freely, but always with a request that they may be returned with the borrower's opinion, candidly expressed in writing, anent the soundness of the views he expresses in support of the different subjects treated of. When that request is not complied with, he takes it for granted that his statements are quite unanswerable. He complained to me, that the minister of an adjoining parish had kept one of his MSS. nearly a year, and at length returned it with a short note, merely apologising for having kept it so long.

To attain my object of gaining all the information I possibly could, respecting Mrs Buchan and her followers, I was obliged to act a different part; although I often found myself at a loss what to say regarding dogmas repugnant to my feelings, more particularly as I was aware, that a single word slightingly or incautiously written, might shut the door against me for ever.

The first time I called on Mr Innes at his own house, I showed him several documents respecting Mrs Buchan, which he did not conceive were in existence; and I gave him to understand, at the same time, that I had been occasionally employed, lately, in collecting all the information I could relating to the society, with a view to publication, if, upon due consideration, I should find the materials collected suitable for that purpose. He seemed surprised, but said, I was certainly at liberty to do so, though any attempt to redeem the character of the founder of that sect, or of any of those who left their homes to follow her faith or practice, from the aspersions that had been cast on them by the world, would be as impossible as to cause the author of sin to do that which was right; and, although I wished to repeat all that had already been said against them, to show that he was not afraid on his own account of my doing so, he would afford me every assistance in his power; in token of which, he gave me a letter to a gentleman in Dumfries, of the following purport :—

"Sir,—I hope you will be so kind as give the bearer, Mr Joseph Train of Castle Douglas, the book containing copies of your grandmother's letters, and a narrative of my own life, while in the society." ..

On presenting this letter to Mr S******, he admitted his having the book in question, and said, if I would only allow him to retain it for a few days, for the purpose of making marginal notes for my guidance, he would hand it to a relation of mine, then residing in Dumfries. To this arrangement I cordially agreed; but, regardless of the most direct and binding promises, he holds it still.

The MS. in question, was written by Andrew Innes about the year 1820, at the request of the late Captain Jones of Brooklands, for the perusal of the late Mr M'Adam of Castledykes, near Dumfries. Andrew expected I would receive the book without any difficulty, but, on finding that was not the case, he wrote me as follows :—

"Crocketford, 21st January 1839

" Sir,

"I received your letter of the 16th, informing me that you have not received the book from Mr S******. I cannot conceive what his design can be for keeping it for one moment, if it is not for the purpose of adulterating the meaning before he parts with it; but any thing he may do in that respect, can do little harm, as I could put all right at the first view, as I have a copy of the whole in my possession. As you are so much interested in seeing some of Mr White's writings or publications, I have sent you his Divine Dictionary, which has been in print upwards of fifty years; and though it contains many things in direct opposition to the religious opinions of the present times, I never yet heard of any person attempting to make the assertions contained in it false, except on the grounds of slander.

"Since John S****** has not given you the book required by my letter, I will employ all my spare time, of which I have now plenty, in writing out for you a sketch of all the essential proceedings of our society since its commencement. . . . . —Yours respectfully,

(Signed) "ANDREW INNES."

So far, therefore, from my design being thwarted by Mr S****** withholding the MS., that circumstance produced quite a different result. Andrew Innes drew up for me a more minute and extended account of the society than he had formerly written. The following communication will show, that the attempt made by another relation of Mrs Buchan, proved also abortive, in persuading Mr Innes that my sole object was to obtain all the information I could respecting the Buchanites, for the purpose of composing a play, in which he, Mrs Buchan, and Mr White, were to be the chief actors; all of whom, like the characters in the "Gentle Shepherd," would probably, ere long, be brought on the stage, for the amusement, perhaps, of his nearest neighbours:—

"Crocketford, 25th Feb 1839.

"Dear Sir,

"The weather has been so very cold of late, that I have been obliged to write for you with my gloves on: as I consider cold a child of the author of death, I therefore use every means in my power to resist its effects. The narrative having pleased you so well, I have filled up the blank book which you left with me also, for your information, with such matter as I thought would be most interesting to you. I will expect to hear your opinion of the whole, and if any thing appears dark or uncertain to you, I will be happy to clear it up.

"You have already seen a specimen of what I have written, for the satisfaction of some of my neighbours, on various subjects; and as I have a number yet beside me which you have not seen, I have sent you herewith a few of them; and I request, particularly, that you give me your opinion of them, especially those I have written concerning *the soul of man*, and *man's nervous system*. You see that I am far from thinking that this generation will not feel a calamity of their own providing, although I have as little desire to see it as Jesus had to see the city of Jerusalem destroyed, when he wept for its fall. I may have my days numbered before these calamities come, as come they will; but I forewarn you all who may see them, that God will have no more hand in them than he had in the destruction of Jerusalem.—From your friend, &c.

"Andrew Innes."

I was thus furnished with eight different essays in one day, and a continuation of the narrative, from which I gained much insight into the peculiar opinions of the writer, and of the Buchanites in general; but the critical notices I was required to give on these writings did not meet his approbation, as he said " I had merely gathered the leaves of the tree, and left the fruit."

The concluding sentence of the preceding letter, evidently alludes to the near approach of the general judgment, which gave poor Andrew so much trouble when lying in the old quarry-hole at Leadhills. The following is not less visionary:—

"Crocketford, 30th April 1839

" My very dear Friend,

" Robert Little has informed me, that you are proposing to bring a gig here the first fine day, to take me to Castle Douglas, merely because I have not been there for a long time. Your kindness has astonished me, from the first day I saw your face, shining like that of Moses when he returned from Mount Sinai,—it was so radiant, that his brethren could not look upon him; or, like Stephen with his angelic countenance before his murderers; or as her's (whose actions you are so desirous to know) was at the great agitation at New Cample. This is the reward I wish you to enjoy, for all your friendship to the old man at Crocketford.

" This I can say in truth, although I have conferred benefits ten times more extensive on others, than the trouble I have taken for you, I never received so much as a pleasant look or a pleasant word from any of them. On that account, you may judge of my feelings on viewing so many superabundant rewards from you. Were it possible for a person to live at the extremity of the earth, in total darkness for several months, you may conceive what the feelings of that person must be, when he saw the first ray of light appearing above the horizon. Such are my feelings at present. The author of my light has been below the horizon for nearly half a century, and how can I avoid being glad at the sight of such a morning-star, as you appear to be at present in my sight?

"I never obtain what I write, till the pen is in my hand; hence you may judge from whom I receive my information. A part of my morning meditation has just come to hand, and I am willing to commit it to paper. The name Joseph led me to Egypt, where Joseph laid up a store for his brethren, and for all the surrounding nations. In like manner, I have pleasure in supposing you to be his brother after the spirit, providing for a famine which is near at hand, and that you are doing so under the influence, and as an instrument in the hands of God. . . . .
—Your friend and well-wisher,

"ANDREW INNES."

Could any thing be more imaginative than this? The singularity of a person, at this distance of time, expressing any curiosity respecting the peculiarities of the sect, seem in a wonderful manner to have rekindled the old man's enthusiasm and poetic fancy. The following fantasy is worthy of Mrs Buchan herself:—

"Crocketford, 17th Feb. 1840.

"MY VERY VERY DEARLY AND DESERVEDLY BELOVED FRIEND,—I received your kind letter of the 11th curt., with the valuable presents, and am highly gratified by your approbation of 'Friend Mother's fireside chitchat,'—by which, in plain words, I mean confidential conversation—about the manners and customs of our society, with which few are now acquainted. I have lost all the companions of my youthful days, who witnessed the wonderful things I have written to you. I am left alone, like the pelican in the wilderness, in appearance, but that is not really the case. *I sleep every night in my Friend Mother's house, and breakfast with her family in the morning. I go there in the capacity of your errand-boy,* and am consequently well-received. Had I your company there for a single meal, you would not envy the guests at the Queen's marriage-feast, of all the rarities and rich sauces in golden dishes. From this you may see, that you are not putting me to any disagreeable trouble on your account.[1]

[1] Such a personal intercourse with the world of spirits, was perhaps never pretended to by any other individual, except the Baron Swedenborg, a Swedish nobleman, who founded the sect called "The New Jerusalem Church." In his "Treatise concerning heaven and hell," he says—" As often as I conversed with angels face to face, it was in their habitations, which are like to our houses on earth, but far more beautiful and magnificent, having rooms, chambers, and apartments, in great variety, as also spacious courts belonging to them, together with

"I am consequently glad to see that you have not forgot your *errand-boy*, as you have given him a new commission; and I have no doubt of his bringing you a good supply of fresh information from the same quarter. Your desire to know how Mr White conducted himself at the great agitation, and during the fast, will be a sufficient introduction to make me welcome; and although I may not get an answer such as you or I may expect, I am sure to get one more profitable to us. From this you may be certain, that when any thing valuable comes to your hands, you have not the old man at Crocketford to thank for it.

"My hand and pen are not sufficient to describe the satisfaction your last letter has given to your sincere friend,

"ANDREW INNES."

Again he wrote me as follows:—

"Crocketford, 14th March 1840.

"MY DEAR DEAR SIR,

"You will easily perceive that I write you more freely, and in a more confidential manner than I have ever done to any other person, because of the frankness and undisguised manner of your inquiries, which has enabled me to enlarge the information

gardens, parterres of flowers, fields, &c., where the angels are formed into societies. They dwell in contiguous habitations, disposed after the manner of our cities, in streets, walks, and squares. I have had the privilege to walk through them, to examine all round about me, and to enter their houses, and this when I was fully awake, having my inward eyes opened."—Evans' Sketch of the Denominations of the Christian World. London edition, 1808, p. 214

to you, much beyond any other person unconnected with the society.

"I have shown you, that the author of our society was actually the very person prophesied of by St John in the twelfth chapter of the Revelation; and that she as amply performed all that he had told concerning her, as Jesus did all that the prophets wrote concerning him. I have also shown you that the principal object that kept us together as a society, was the sense of her being what Mr White represented her to be in his Divine Dictionary, and in his other writings, and to ourselves; and the prospect of obtaining the reward promised by Christ to his faithful followers who endured to the end—that was, personal translation;—and I have shown you the supernatural power that always attended us, especially from the time of our leaving Irvine till the fast, but more particularly at that time;—and I have also shown you that the disappointment of the disciples of Jesus was as to inheriting a wordly kingdom, which they expected by him until he expired on the cross.

"It is the confidence that I had, and still have, of you benefiting by this information, that has enabled me to write these things to you, which is not so much as hinted at in my writings to any one else unconnected with the society; but you may require additional light, to see through all the things that are already fulfilled to the utmost extent, and are as clear to me as the beams of the sun can make them, because I was both eye and ear witness to them.—I am yours, &c.

(Signed) "ANDREW INNES."

It might well be supposed, that age had enfeebled the intellect and darkened the understanding of the writer of this letter. But the reader of the preceding pages may have observed, that Andrew Innes was a religious enthusiast from his youth. It was he who converted to the Buchanite faith all the people of Muthill, who joined the society at Irvine; but his whimsies so far out-rivalled, in extravagance, those entertained by even the founder of the sect and her assistant White, that, when leaving the society at New Cample, it will be recollected he was ordered by the latter not to return without a certificate from his parish minister as to the sanity of his mind—a point which might again have been strongly questioned at the time he proposed with James Sanders, Mrs Buchan's son-in-law, to commence another fast of forty days, in order to prepare himself for heaven. He was the apostle dispatched on all important missions; or, in his own words, was really "the errand-boy" of the society; though, in the preceding letter, he assumes, under that title, the character and office of an angel. We were evidently playing at cross-purposes. His sole aim was, to induce me to believe in his fanatical notions—mine was, to gain a thorough knowledge of the faith and practice of Mrs Buchan and her deluded followers: but, just at the time he was about to reveal to me so many of her fireside secrets, one rash movement of my ardour in this pursuit, put a total stop to the intended disclosures, and had nearly put a period to any further intercourse between us.

Having received all the information to be got respecting the fast of forty days, I ventured to send him an extract from "Blackwood's Magazine" for May 1820, and another from the "Castle-Douglas Miscellany" for March 1826, respecting Lady Buchan's heavenward flight, with an accompanying letter, apologising for doing so, on account of that subject not having been mentioned in any of the writings with which he had favoured me. To this communication he replied—" I think you might have been satisfied with what I wrote you respecting Friend Mother. If I were to employ my time in confuting false assertions like those you have sent me, I might write to the end of my life, without producing any good effect. *I hope a more suitable time will arrive in your day, for publishing Friend Mother's life;* but the prospect of my witnessing it, is now small. This may be considered as a fear on my part, for having written the narrative of the society now in your possession; but I defy all the sons of men to contradict a single sentence of what I have written. Friend Mother's character has been represented in the blackest colours already; but she is now out of the reach of her enemies, some of whom would, I dare say, like John Gibson, *vent their ill-will on her grave, if they knew where to find it.*"

I was aware that the allusion to the grave of Mrs Buchan, was jeeringly made in a moment of irritation, to check my prying further into the secrets of the society than he thought proper to declare; but I knew more of the interment of his Friend Mother than Andrew was aware of. So watchful was the public, on the death of Mrs Buchan, lest her remains should pollute any of the neighbouring churchyards, that the sheriff, as formerly stated, deemed it prudent, for the preservation of the peace of the country, to meet Mr White by appointment at midnight, near Auchengibbert. What follows, falls now to be related.

On arriving at the appointed place, Sir Alexander Gordon met Mr White and George Hill, and proceeded forthwith to Kirkgunzeon churchyard, a distance of three miles, where they arrived by break of day. White informed the sheriff, that he and his companion were the only persons present at the interment of Mrs Buchan, and were the only individuals that knew the exact place where she was laid; that they had taken advantage of a lately-made grave; and, the better to ensure concealment, that they had raised the coffin, and placed that of Mrs Buchan beneath it. On this violated grave being pointed out to Sir Alexander, he caused it to be again opened, and both coffins taken out; when laid on the sward, and the lids removed, he examined the contents himself. The coffin first disinterred, contained the body of a man; which he ascertained by passing one of his fingers along the lower part of the face to feel the beard; the other that of a woman carefully packed in feathers, which the sheriff instantly recognised as the remains of Mrs Buchan, having frequently seen her when in life.

These particulars remained a profound secret for at least thirty years, and would probably have remained so for ever, had not Sir Alexander Gordon, one evening shortly before his death, related to a party of friends all the incidents just mentioned, to one of whom I am obliged for the information. Sir Alexander having been dead several years, I applied to his son, Colonel James Gordon of Balcary, on this subject, and am happy to have it in my power to add his confirmation to the previous statement:—

"Balcary, 22d April 1840.

" Sir,

" I was in Edinburgh attending the college at the time of Mrs Buchan's death, but my sister says your account of my father having gone, as sheriff, with an officer, during the night, accompanied by the Buchanite minister Mr White, to Kirkgunzeon churchyard, is correct. The frenzy of the people was such, that Mr White was in danger of being maltreated had he appeared in public at that time, on which account he undertook to show my father Mrs Buchan's body in that churchyard at night, her followers having carried it there, and buried it by opening a late-made grave, and placing her under the other coffin. My father left Greenlaw at night, that he might be at the grave by break of day, before any person would have risen. He was shown the grave, saw it opened, and both coffins taken out, and the contents examined. She was in the lower one, packed in feathers; both coffins were replaced in the grave before any of the neighbours were up.

"I recollect hearing my father mentioning all these particulars, many years after the occurrence. . . .
(Signed) "JAMES GORDON."

This discovery plainly shows White to have been both a hypocrite and an impostor. He saw Mrs Buchan pay the common debt of nature, and laid her head in the grave; yet he had the effrontery and duplicity to assure even those persons, who by his instrumentality, had been alienated from the simplicity of Divine truth, that the idol of their folly had ascended to heaven in his presence. Thinking all the circumstances attending Mrs Buchan's *first* funeral could not be wholly unknown to Andrew Innes, and being anxious to elicit from him whatever information he might possess on the subject, I forwarded Colonel Gordon's letter to him, enclosed in a sketch of all the particulars that led to that communication; but, from his answer received in course of post, I found I had been treading on forbidden ground:—

"Crocketford, 10th June 1840

"DEAR SIR,

"With respect to your request concerning my opinion of the account of Colonel Gordon as to the burial-place of Friend Mother, it would be deemed presumption in me to express a doubt upon the information you have already received from persons of the sheriff's own family, who heard it at different times from his own mouth, and confirmed by others who received it in the same indisputable manner.

All I can say is, that the statement is altogether new to me, for I never heard of her having been buried either in Kirkgunzeon kirkyard, or in any other, nor of her having been buried under another coffin, as the Colonel says; but all this is now of very little importance. It is plenty for me to know, that the angels who attended her when on earth, will know where to find her at the second coming of the Lord, when the tares shall be separated from the wheat upon earth, as the sheep were from the goats in heaven at the ascension of Jesus.

"You have been fortunate in getting such a full account of Friend Mother before my sight failed, as I could not write it now; but I would like to see what you have taken from my writings. I will pay attention to returning the book in due time; and your complying with this request will be remembered, with other favours, by your old feeble correspondent,

"ANDREW INNES."

The MS. book here referred to, contains the narrative of the society, from which extracts have been so often given in the course of this sketch, with copies of the letters I had received from him; also extracts from his essays, and from Mrs Buchan's communications, with a copy of every account or incidental notice of the Buchanites which I had been able to procure from the various publications in which they appeared.

These papers being classed, titled, and paged

throughout, with a table of contents, and an introduction, and being handsomely bound, formed a respectable volume; but my friend did not wish to see his writings in such company. I plainly perceived, by the preceding letter, that he was not in his usual tranquil state of mind; and, fearing lest my discovery of the burial-place of Mrs Buchan might be the cause of it, and wishing to give him as little pain as possible on such an important point of his faith, I instantly forwarded the book he wished, and in a day or two afterwards proceeded personally to Crocketford, merely to ascertain that he was not indisposed, and to converse with him on the subject of Colonel Gordon's letter.

Although the day was very hot, I found him wrapped in his old plaid-cloak, seated by a strong peat fire; and I had scarcely placed myself on my usual seat beside him, when he said—" You have really been very active in striving to find out Friend Mother's grave—you will surely be satisfied now." Thinking he had spoken in a jocular manner, I replied, that I was still anxious to learn further particulars of Friend Mother's fireside, with which he had kindly promised to furnish me. On which he hastily rejoined, " I have not another word to communicate on the subject, and I think you may be well content with the information you have already received." He then asked me, if I had kept a copy of Colonel Gordon's letter. I told him I had not, as I thought there was not much fear of my losing the original, as I considered it safe while in his hands; and it, being a document of singular importance, I would preserve it carefully.

Observing that I did not wish to part with it, he said, "The letter is of great importance to me, and cannot be of any to you; but as you want it, there it is"—at the same time handing it to me. I asked him, if a certified copy would answer his purpose? if not, I would keep such a copy myself, and return the original to him. This offer he declined, saying, if there was to be any copying in the matter, I might keep it altogether.

I was more surprised, however, to find, that he had cut up my manuscript, and had not only taken out every line of his own writing, but had interlined a great part of mine with very singular remarks. He gave as his reason for doing so, that I had made short extracts only from Mrs Buchan's letters and his essays; whereas, I had copied every thing I could find that appeared to be against her or the society, at full length; and as the book appeared to be quite ready for the press, he was resolved to deprive me of his part of it.

I had often heard of his being a very captious person, but had not seen any thing previously to warrant my belief in the character ascribed to him.[1]

[1] One instance may be mentioned of the ungovernable temper of the old man: A dispute having arisen between him and one of his tenants in the village of Crocketford, respecting the fruit of a cherry-tree which was trained up against the gable of the tenant's house :— "I let you the house and garden only," said Andrew; "but the tree is not in the garden, and it was never mentioned in our bargain; therefore, you have no right to the fruit of it." "But my kitchen

However, as I supposed myself to have been the cause of his irritation in this instance, I did all in my power to allay his anger, by assuring him that he was quite mistaken as to my having any intention of publishing the manuscript in the form in which he had seen it; and that the materials it contained, were arranged merely for my own convenience, when drawing up my intended sketch of the society, for which purpose he had placed these materials at my disposal.[1] But it was not till I had urged upon his mind the impropriety of withholding the narrative which he had frankly given to me, and the letters I had received from him by post, that he reluctantly returned to me these documents. These papers I

fire," rejoined the tenant, "being directly behind the tree, the intervening wall is thereby so warmed, as greatly to promote the vegetation and fruit of your tree at my expense." Andrew, having an axe in his hand, struck the trunk of the tree with the intention of cutting it down, rather than submit to any reasoning on the subject, and was about to strike it again, when the tenant arrested his hand, saying,—"Stop, that is only taking advantage of yourself. I will rather relinquish my claim, than see your property thus destroyed." As if struck with this generous concession, Andrew desisted, and walked away, saying, "If you think you have a right to the fruit, take it."

[1] "You will find, as I told you in a former letter, that the publishing of her (Mrs Buchan) true character could only be of service to some writer of novels or other new publications; and though I had indulged you in all that you required, and, I suppose, more than you expected, it was without hope of redeeming her character, or that of any person that was with her, in the view of the world at large,—a thing I consider as impossible as to make the author of sin do that which is right. Yet, lest you should consider me afraid of the consequences, I leave you at full liberty to publish what you think proper, interrupting your friendly intercourse with your friend and well-wisher,

(Signed) " ANDREW INNES."

immediately got bound anew; and, certainly, the interest of the book is not lessened by the interlineations alluded to.[1]

Andrew looked forward with intense anxiety to the awful period of Friend Mother's advent from heaven, to convince the faithless world of its error, in supposing her to be one of the false prophets foretold in the Old Testament book of Deuteronomy. The savings of many years, converted into gold, and bound up in an old thread stocking, he placed in the hands of his old and valued friend, Alexander Cavet of Little Larg, under certain injunctions, lest his upward flight might be retarded, by having such a weight of worldly dross in his possession. But the most extended period predicted for that great event, came and passed away. The sun continued to rise and set as formerly, and though Mrs Buchan did not appear at Crocketford, strange to say, the faith of Andrew Innes, in her divinity and predictions, appeared in nowise shaken.

A few weeks after the time of Luckie's expected advent, the pastor of a religious sect, thinly spread over Kirkcudbrightshire, to whom the history of Mrs Buchan, and most of the persons who followed her from Irvine, was well known, called on Andrew Innes, whilst on one of his peregrinations amongst his flock, expecting to find him in great tribulation for having been led astray from the right path,

---

[1] This is the MS. alluded to in the History of Galloway, vol. ii. chap. 8, by the Rev. William Mackenzie, now minister of Skirling

during such a lengthened period of his life, by the fantasies and false pretensions of a fanatical woman, and willing to return to the bosom of the church. But as soon as the old man perceived the object of his visit, he ordered him instantly to quit the house, saying, " When I want your spiritual advice, sir, I will send for you. In the mean time, I will not listen to a word you can say on the subject you have advanced, as I am as firm in the belief at present, of the divine mission of Mrs Buchan, as at any former period of my life."

Nearly a year after this interview had taken place, I had also a strong proof of his unshaken belief in the return of Mrs Buchan. On my naming to him the large sum for which an eminent banker in London had compounded with government as his quota of the income-tax, for the three years for which the act had been passed, he hastily replied, " Ah! before the end of that time, there will be no income tax required; people will not work for wages then."

He subsequently became more explicit. In a letter which I received from him, dated 20th August 1843, he writes thus:—" I can assure you, from Christ's own words, that his second coming will be in this present year, 1843, (be not surprised at this; although new, it is true,) and I wish you to have then a spoon and a seat at the great banquet-table, beside those who will not taste of death."

As this appeared to be merely another attempt to induce me to become a convert to the religious opinions of my old acquaintance, I took no notice of the prophecy, and we continued our intercourse as formerly.

Not being satisfied with the answer of Andrew to my letter of the 22d April 1840, enclosing that of Colonel Gordon of Balcary, as in that communication he affirmed that he was not aware of Luckie Buchan having been buried in the kirkyard of Kirkgunzeon, I mentioned this circumstance to Mr Cavet of Little Larg, who, from his infancy upwards, had been well acquainted with, and much respected by, the people of Larghill, who were his immediate neighbours. He was, besides, the intimate personal friend of Andrew Innes, and was consulted by him on all important occasions. Mr Cavet did not doubt the truth of Andrew's statement to me of his ignorance of Mrs Buchan having been buried in the kirkyard of Kirkgunzeon, but accounted for it, from the circumstance of his being always at variance with Mr White, after being expelled from the society during the " Great Fast of Forty Days" at Closeburn. Though Andrew returned to the society, in compliance with the wishes of Luckie Buchan, Mr White kept him in the dark as much as he possibly could, in all matters connected with the affairs of their little community; and, after the death of the founder of their sect, the outbreaking of their discord, as has been seen, led to a disruption of their body at Auchengibbert.

Mr Cavet said, that, on the night after the sheriff had inspected the remains of Mrs Buchan in the dormitory of the dead, at Kirkgunzeon, Duncan Robertson and George Hill, assisted by Mr White, removed her remains thence to Auchengibbert, where they were deposited beneath the kitchen hearthstone. As soon as Mr White and his adherents left Auchengibbert for America, Andrew Innes took possession of the corpse of Mrs Buchan, removed it by night to his new residence at Larghill; and with all possible privacy, several years afterwards, when this little band of enthusiasts were about to remove to their own property at Crocketford, the bones of old Luckie were deposited in a large chest, generally used for the purpose of holding the spare blankets of the society. This *kist*, with the bones, was removed from Larghill to the Buchanite house at Crocketford, and there placed in the dark closet formerly mentioned. Here it was allowed to remain, till Mrs Goldie left the society, and returned to Dumfries; when, lest she might inform her nephew of his grandmother's bones being yet above ground, and thus possibly endanger the peace of the society, it was removed to a cellar, or *tofall*, in the ground behind the workshop. This removal took place the night preceeding that on which Mr S****** made the search already mentioned in this little work. Had he, therefore, made his survey of the suspected place a day sooner, he would have found his grandmother's remains in the place pointed out to him by his aunt.

This little charnel-house being attached to the end of the dwelling-house, in which was the bed-closet of Andrew Innes, and in which he generally sat when not engaged in out-door work, the bones in the cell were directly opposite the back of the bedroom fire, as was supposed for the purpose of keeping them dry; but twice every day in the year, with the greatest regularity, he heated a flannel cloth at his fire, and then pushed it with the poker through a hole in the wall at the back of the grate, made for that purpose, whence the cloth fell into the rude coffin where the skeleton lay. He then went out at a back door in his bedroom, removed the former flannel, and carefully spread that newly heated over the skeleton. "This," my informant (who was for a long time his only personal attendant) says, "he invariably performed, with as much privacy as if his life solely depended on the concealment of these bones." The flannel last removed from the bones, he always bound round his head when going to bed at night, under the superstitious belief that it was a preventive from every ill by which mankind is afflicted.

The enthusiastic old man spent a certain time daily beside the remains of his deceased mistress, evidently in the performance of some peculiar devotion. To these reveries he evidently alludes in his letter on the 17th February 1840, where he says—"I sleep every night in Friend Mother's house, and breakfast every morning with her family."

As the 29th March 1841 drew nigh, the expiry of the full time within which Mrs Buchan declared she would return to the world, he spent much time beside the bones, in the language of Scripture, "with his loins girded, and his lamp burning," ready for that important crisis, when, in the twinkling of an eye, he should burst the bonds of mortality, and find himself in the presence of her whom he had so highly honoured and adored. Disappointment came, but it did not blast his hopes; for, in the peculiar tenets of his devotion, Andrew Innes seemingly stood alone in the world, uncountenanced even by his partner Katherine Gardner. This woman, during the long period of fifty-eight years, in which she had resided in Galloway, was never known to have attended any place of worship. At Crocketford, she refrained from turning her spinning-wheel on the Sabbath-day, but whether she did so in obedience to the divine command, or only in compliance with the example set by her religious neighbours, was known only to herself.

She was generally considered by the public, as being one of the society of Buchanites, but according to her husband, Andrew Innes, she had no claim to that distinction. In the summer of the year 1845, she became bed-ridden, and died in the November following. During her last illness, the only worldly anxiety manifested by her was, that she might be soon able to get out of bed again, to see that the wants of Andrew were properly attended to. She had an old chest of drawers, which, immediately before her death, she bequeathed to the woman who attended her, saying, with her last breath, "Oh, be careful of Andrew; he sits with his feet on the ribs of the grate, which has fashed me muckle. If the timber soles of his clogs was to tak fire, his feet and legs micht be roasted, before he could shift the chair, or ony body come to his assistance."

When the recovery of old Katie had become hopeless, I requested of Andrew Innes to be invited to her funeral, when that should happen; and I would have attended, although at the distance of nine miles, merely for the purpose of noting the occurrence of any peculiarity in the performance of the funeral obsequies; but a few days after the funeral, I received a letter from Andrew, of which the following is a copy:—

"Crocketford, 1st December 1845.

"DEAR SIR,

"I have no doubt but you will have heard of Katherine's death, and would be ready to suppose me negligent in not sending you notice sooner, as you expressed a wish to be present at the funeral; but I hope my stating a few facts, will relieve you from that apprehension. The cold frosty winds at the beginning of last month, almost deprived me of the use of my limbs, which, you know, are both weakly at any time, and the frosty wind also seized my head with such a giddiness upon Monday last, that I required more help than usual to support me standing, till my clothes were put on; on Tuesday I was worse. On Wednesday, Katherine died; and I fixed Friday for burying her, at which time I could not walk a step without the assistance of two persons,— one holding me up at each side. I only invited a few persons; and you know they had not far to carry her to the grave. I did not forget your request, but really I was not able to write, and this is the first attempt I have made to hold a pen since.

"You may rest assured that I have given you in the narrative, and since, a true account of all matters connected with the society, and with its author, except a few circumstances connected with our fast of forty days, which I could not well describe, and which no one, that was not personally present, could comprehend. . . . . .

"This statement of unvarnished facts, I bid defiance to either her enemies or mine to contradict. I have always believed Friend Mother to be as represented by Mr White in his Divine Dictionary; and, through her, I have looked forward to personal translation, without tasting death —Yours, &c."

The fallacy of such a faith will immediately appear.

The enfeebled frame of this singular old man sustained such a shock by the death of his ancient helpmate, that his remaining health and bodily strength declined rapidly. I visited him on 31st December 1845: he was then very weak, and spoke seemingly with difficulty; a few days afterwards he fell, when outside, attempting to visit the graveyard. On the 15th January, in answer to some inquiries which I had made respecting his health, a friend wrote thus :—" Mr Innes has got the better of his fall, but I think his health is fast giving way, and that he is entering into a state of mixed consumption and dropsy, which I fear will cut him off ere long." Four days later I received a note, from which the following is an extract:—

"I write you this in a hurry, merely to inform you, that Mr Innes died this morning at seven o'clock, sitting in his arm-chair, seemingly without pain.

"The demise of no other individual in this locality could have caused such a sensation as the death of Andrew Innes, it being generally known that he expected to be translated to heaven; but when the proof came that he was not exempted from the general lot of humanity, all his wild pretensions in that respect were seen to have been only the ravings of a disordered mind. This was the more singular, as he was, except on religious subjects, a staid sensible man."

A valued correspondent, very shortly before his demise, sent him the following queries on articles of the Buchanite faith, merely to ascertain on what grounds he had discontinued the observation of certain rules laid down to the society by Mrs Buchan, and for ascertaining the articles of his faith at the time of his death:—

Questions for Mr Innes.

"1. If Friend Mother be the woman spoken of in Revelations xii., how do you explain her flight into the wilderness, and nourishment there from the face of the serpent, for a time, times, and half a time, or 1260 days? What do you hold those times to mean

—and how do you apply them to Friend Mother's case?

"2. Friend Mother being a good woman, her spiritual births behoved to be good also. How, then, can you call such a man as Mr White her child? and how can you hold him as having been caught up to God, and His throne, which he assuredly never was—it being Christ alone who has ascended, or ever shall ascend, to that throne, on which He reigns, and shall reign, without a rival?

"3. Friend Mother having been continually speaking of, and instructing the society in, spiritual things, it cannot be but that Mr Innes remembers many of those things, consisting both of remarkable sayings, and expositions of Scripture. Will Mr Innes, therefore, be so good as recall and write down as many of these as he can?

"4. Friend Mother, in all her letters, inculcates the proper Christian exercise of prayer and praise. Did she and the society follow in practice, what she thus inculcates in her letters? and if not, for what reason, seeing that the Lord and all his apostles inculcate the same things?"

The following answers to the above queries, appear to have been about the very last production of his pen:—

Answers by Mr Innes.

"Your first question is respecting her flight into the wilderness, and her being there 1260 days. I consider her flight into the wilderness in two stages, like Israel's captivity to Babylon. The first, when carried to Stewarton by a mob, and banished the next day by Irvine magistrates, when she went to Muthill, and returned several months after, and was banished a second time from Irvine in the month of May following, to Closeburn, where she remained three years, without the certainty of one single night's possession, before the mob threatened her with treatment such as she received in Irvine; and after a law protection was given her by the circuit court, she was kept under the fear of being burnt alive every night she remained in that place. Her first flight was in the month of October in 1783, as you may see by the date of her letters from Muthill: and she obtained a residence in Auchengibbert at Whitsunday 1787; so you may calculate if the days and years you mention, be contained in that period, for I can assure you I was so well supplied with so much better proof, that it never entered my mind to think of it as a proof.

"Your second question, is respecting the certainty of her divine original, or spiritual birth; and that is a question that I answer with great confidence and pleasure also. And I give you the words that proceeded from her own mouth for my authority. She often said, that she sprung, or was made, of that blood that was scattered at the foot of Christ's cross, and was on that account as nearly connected with the second Adam, as Eve was to the first. I know I am leading you into deep waters here, yet you having nothing to fear, for he that can lead you in, can support you, or keep you from drowning."

The literal copy of the remainder of the answers, is here lost; but the following is a faithful abstract of their contents:—That Mrs Buchan bringing forth a man child, who was caught up to God and His throne, to rule all nations with a rod of iron, was figurative, and spiritually fulfilled in Mr White's adoption of her views, and thus getting seated in the hearts of her children or followers, whose hearts unitedly constituted the throne of God; and that Mr White's ruling all nations with a rod of iron, was also fulfilled in his subsequent tyrannical conduct, both towards Mrs Buchan and them—they, her followers, symbolising the nations of the millenial reign, as the Jewish patriarchs symbolised the twelve tribes, and the apostles the Christians.

The third question was passed by with but this brief observation—that Friend Mother's acts spoke far more eloquently than her words, and that both her words and acts must be detailed with due caution, to such only as have light enough to receive and understand them!

Question fourth elicited the response, that Friend Mother's and the society's whole life, being but one continued expressive act of both prayer and praise, she and they needed not to engage in outward vocal formalities to that effect, like others who walked less perfectly; and that, though it was true enough that both Christ and his apostles prayed and praised, and inculcated the like duties upon their followers—yet, their dispensation being much lower than that which Friend Mother began, such things consequently became as unsuitable to this new higher dispensation, as the old Jewish sacrifices were to the Christian economy, which did them away. But the discrepancy between this view, and the fact of Mrs Buchan inculcating both prayer and praise in her letters, was passed by!

It was held to be a great point by Andrew, that the members of his confraternity should display much firmness and imperturbability during their last illness; as that, in his opinion, afforded a strong proof of the truth of their religion, shining through so conclusive a triumph of their faith. And on this account, he was in the habit of watching all their deathbeds, anxiously noting their expressions and demeanour, and pointing out to favourable attention, such as he thought orthodox and becoming, or accounting for such as he disapproved, on the score of fleshly weakness, or temporary mental wandering. A striking instance of this has already been narrated in the case of Duncan Robertson; and when his own sister, Peggy Jones, died, she was kept from leaping over the Buchanite wall in precisely the same manner; for Peggy had, through means of the nurse got in to attend her, managed to have an elder of the established church smuggled up stairs into her apartment in order to pray with her; but Andrew detected something strange going forward immediately, and, hastening up stairs, made such a display of temper, as caused his sister to beg that what so ruffled him, might not be persisted in on her account—a fine act of sisterly charity and submission, in a moment so earnest and all-important. His wife, old Katie, escaped better when dying, through his greatly increased deafness and blindness; yet, in her case also, many an act and word did he see and hear, that caused him to shake his head and groan inwardly; for the fact is, she was possessed of great native sincerity and downrightness of character, which perhaps was the cause of her never melting so thoroughly into the society as others, so that the outside, at which she was constantly kept, made her familiar with many little misfortunes, which took off the fiery edge of fanaticism, and gave her a kindly breadth and softness of spirit, that shed a peaceful air of piety and resignation over her deathbed, not at all unique, and singular and exclusive enough to please her husband. As was naturally to be expected, from the habit he had thus acquired, when the time came to adjust his own mantle and fall, a singular contest took place within him for a little, as to whether he should really yield himself up to enact the dying man's part, or still cling to his darling hope of translation without death. But one very severe night's illness, immediately thereafter, so strained and cracked all the timbers and cords of his clay vessel, as to make him exclaim that it was all over with him—that he could stand very few more like it, but must soon give way, as he now recognised what hand it was that had him in its grasp, indeed. From that moment, he affected great coolness and self-possession; re affirmed, to those who asked him, his peculiar dogmas; busied himself with arrangements concerning his papers, clothes, and property; held long conversations with those admitted to see him; and ventured, at length, to utter a prophecy, that, on the morning of the third day from that on which he thus became oracular, he would expire— which actually came to pass!

Only four days before this event, the unaltered devotee sent for three of his friends, and gave them particular directions that the box, containing the remains of Mrs Buchan, should be interred in the same grave as himself; and in order to have this accomplished with all possible privacy, he directed that his grave should be made on the day previous to his interment, and on the morning of his funeral, at cock-crowing, they were to remove the box containing the remains of Mrs Buchan to the grave, and after depositing it there, to cover the rude coffin with a few shovels full of the bottom mould, and press it so as to give it the appearance of being the real bottom of the grave, for the purpose of effectually concealing from those who attended his funeral, what had become of the remains of his Friend Mother. But the period had arrived when this secret could be no longer kept from the public. The three friends, who had undertaken this duty, being convinced of this, thought it most prudent to conduct the funeral of Andrew and his mistress openly. They, therefore, permitted several of their friends to inspect the rudely-made coffin of Mrs Buchan, and its contents, before removing it from the house for interment; one of whom favoured me, on the same day, with a letter, from which I make the following extract:—

"The coffin, or packing-box, as it may with more propriety be called, as there has never been plane or paint on the wood, is nearly six feet long, and old Luckie's remains occupy nearly the whole length of it. The skin is dark brown, and is like parchment cemented to the bones.* There is black hair, two inches in length, on the hinder part of the skull, and there are two teeth in the mouth; the arms and hands of the skeleton are entire, but the nose, eyes, and feet, are gone. It is laid on straw, with a piece of an old blanket spread across the chest."

In compliance with Andrew's special directions, the coffin was laid in the grave along with his own in the kailyard, on the left flank of the line of the graves of his former associates, and not more than two feet from the back wall of his former bed-room. The villagers crowded to the place of interment, to witness this unique spectacle. As the coffins were lowered into the grave, an expression of melancholy, contempt, or disgust, was seen in every countenance, but a sigh was not heard, nor a tear shed, over the last resting-place of the infatuated Andrew.

Such was the rise, progress, decline, and extinc-

---

* It was the intense heat of the peat fire on the hearth-flag of the kitchen of the farm-house of Auchengibbert, under which the remains of Mrs Buchan were deposited from April 1791 to July of the subsequent year, that scorched her skin, and gave it thus the consistency of parchment

tion, of this little knot of enthusiasts. Their errors have, I trust, been made so apparent, that the readers of the preceding pages may recall to mind, as condemnatory of their blasphemous pretensions, the following lines of Dr Beattie:—

> "One little part we dimly scan,
>   Through the dark medium of life's feverish dream,
> Yet dare arraign the whole stupendous plan,
>   If but that little part incongruous seem.
> O! then renounce that impious self-esteem,
>   That aims to trace the secrets of the skies;
> For thou art but of dust—be humble, and be wise."

APPENDIX.

NOTE 1.

Account of the Buchanites, from a manuscript of the late Dr Richmond, minister of Irvine, kindly communicated by his son, the Rev. John Richmond, minister of Southdean in Roxburghshire.

SOME years ago, upon the death of Mr Jack, Relief minister of this place, that congregation made choice of Mr White to be his successor. Mr White being called to assist at a sacrament in the neighbourhood of Glasgow, Mrs Buchan had an opportunity of hearing him; and, captivated it would appear by his oratory, she communicated to him, by letter, the flattering account of his being the first minister who, as yet, had spoken effectually to her heart, expressing, at the same time, a desire to visit him at Irvine, that she might be further confirmed in the faith. This letter he showed to some of his people, who gave her a very welcome reception, and, from her heavenly conversation and extraordinary gifts, they began to consider her as a very valuable acquisition to their party. Religion was the constant topic of her conversation. In all companies, and upon all occasions, she introduced it. Her time was wholly occupied in visiting from house to house, in making family worship, solving doubts, answering questions, and expounding the Scriptures. At length, however, some of the congregation began to entertain suspicions of the orthodoxy of her principles, all of which had been implicitly imbibed by their minister; they expressed dissatisfaction with his ministry, and desired him to dismiss *her* as a dangerous person. He refused to comply with their request ; they threatened to libel him. Still he remained firm to her interests, and was supported by some of the most wealthy of his hearers.

They drew up a paper, containing what they supposed to be his principles and hers, and desired him to declare whether they *were* his principles. He acknowledged that they were, and readily subscribed them as such. Upon this, they carried the matter before the presbytery, who thought proper to depose him from the office of the ministry. He returned to Irvine, accompanied by his adherents, delivered up the keys of his church, and preached for some time in a tent, and afterwards in his own house. The curiosity of the public was excited, and many frequented his meetings. Strange accounts were given of their doctrines and manner of worship. They usually met in the night time, and were instructed by the pretended prophetess. She gave herself out to be the woman spoken of in the 12th chapter of the Revelation, and that Mr White was the man-child she had brought forth. This, and some other blasphemies she uttered, drew upon her party and herself the indignation of the populace. Idle persons, at different times, assembled in a tumultuous manner, surrounded he house, broke the windows and furniture, and would have proceeded to greater extremities, had it not been for the interposition of the magistrates. After repeated applications from several members of the Relief congregation to have her apprehended, and proceeded against as a blasphemer, the magistrates thought it prudent to dismiss her from the place, which was accordingly done, May 1784. To protect her from insult, they accompanied her for a mile out town ; but, notwithstanding all their efforts, she was grossly insulted by the mob, thrown into ditches, and otherwise ill-used all the way.

She took up her residence that night, in company with some of her followers, in the neighbourhood of Kilmaurs ; and, being joined by Mr White and others in the morning, proceeded on her way to Mauchline, and from thence to Cumnock and Closeburn. They sung as they went, and said that they were going to the " New Jerusalem." Since that time, many of them have returned, and, upon their publicly renouncing their former errors, were admitted members of the *established church*, though it is remarkable that the most, if not the whole of these deluded people, were formerly sectarians.

I have seen a genuine account of Mrs Buchan's death, from a person on the spot. They attempted, it would appear, to carry on the delusion to the last. She had given out that she was to rise again in a few days; this event they accordingly looked for. Mr White and one of his associates visited her corpse, which lay in a barn, twice every day for some time. On the fifth day, they intimated that they had discovered symptoms of returning life; and on the morning of the sixth day, they gave out that she was ascended The grave-clothes were accordingly left in the coffin, and the body had disappeared. Doubts, however, having arisen in the minds of her own relatives, they caused search to be made, and the body was at last found in a pit, that had been hastily dug for its reception in an adjoining field.

NOTE 2.

Communication by William Ayton, Esq. of Hamilton, the celebrated agricultural writer, addressed to his son, a respectable solicitor in Hamilton.

Dear Robert,

Mr Train will probably know, that the inhabitants of Ayrshire not only made a figure in the unhappy disputes between the Episcopalians and Presbyterians in the 16th century, but have, even since the settlement in 1688, been fully as clamorous about religion, as people in any other district in Britain. Mr M'Millan disliked the Revolution settlement, because it did not limit religion to the opinions of the Covenanters; and he became a sort of apostle of that party, and had a good many followers, which form a respectable party to this day. The Erskines became the apostles of the Secession church in 1733; and, in fifteen years afterwards, Mr Gibb became the apostle of the Antiburgher section, and the Erskines and Mr Fisher took the lead among the other half of the Secession church. Mr Whitefield from America next started for a party, and made a good deal of noise for a few years, and sowed the seeds of the Relief sectarians. And as all these parties scolded, not only the national church, but each other, in numerous pamphlets, and thundered violence upon all parties except their own, in their sermons, it would appear that Mrs Buchan had become smitten with the ambition of also becoming the leader of a party, which she imagined she could conduct to heaven by way of Dumfries or Galloway. And she had the address, it seems, to get a Relief clergyman, and a considerable portion of his congregation, to follow her for forty miles, and for several months, expecting every day to reach that happy region.

An occurrence of this kind well merits attention, and ought to be well investigated, for the use of posterity; but all that I know about it is, that I saw them when in *transitu* near Kilmarnock. They went by Logan House on their way heavenward, and Mr Logan, having a few day's before offended some of his neighbours about some parochial matters, he, on seeing a crowd approaching his house, imagining a mob had been raised against him, concealed himself in a plantation of firs, and sent a servant to meet the crowd, and learn what they wanted. The servant soon returned, and told his master that the people said they had come from Irvine, and were going to heaven, and wanted nothing with any one. This relieved the laird of his fears about a mob, and he remarked to his servant, that he was happy to find that Logan House stood on the road to that happy country, a thing he had never known before.

In the month of June 1784, when on my way to England, I found that the party were lodging in a barn, at a farm-house near Thornhill in the county of Dumfries, and I had the curiosity to wait upon them, chiefly to see Mrs Buchan and Mr White, who were so much talked about at that time. As soon as I entered the barn, Mr White presented himself, with Mrs Buchan at his elbow, demanding what I wanted ? I had some difficulty to answer the question; but said, that on passing so near them, I had taken the liberty to call and see people I had heard so much spoken about, and wanted nothing particular. Mr White seemed rather offended at my intrusion; and Mrs Buchan said, rather smartly, if I had any thing to say, she was ready to answer me, and if I wanted nothing with any of them, I might go about my business. on which I retired. The men seemed to be all idle; but some of the females were sewing their clothes, and others cooking. I noticed that there were several handsome, good-looking young women among them, but all of the lower orders.

I happened to be all night in Penpont, in that neighbourhood, a year or two after, when the landlord told me, that when the Buchanites were near Thornhill, the Rev. Mr Fairlie, a Cameronian minister, came to preach at Penpont, and lodged at his house, and that he talked much about them, and particularly about Mr White, and wished to call upon him, that he might be the means of reclaiming him from his errors. The landlord told Mr Fairlie, that it was needless to trouble himself about these people; but he did go with Mr Fairlie to her residence. On calling for Mr White, Mrs Buchan appeared; but, after much delay, the former came forth in a blustering way, and demanded what they wanted Mr Fairlie told him that he had heard strange accounts about his principles and conduct, and leaving his congregation and staying with Mrs Buchan and others, at a distance from their homes, and he added, " I beg you would explain yourself." On which Mr White, in a voice more befitting the stage than the pulpit, roared out, " I am the way, the truth, and the life; none can come unto the Father, but by me." On hearing this, Mr Fairlie turned round his horse, and said, "Farewell, Mr White—farewell, sir—farewell," and the conversation between them ended.

I do not remember any more anecdotes of these parties; but you may assure Mr Train that what I have stated here are facts.—I am, &c.

WILLIAM AYTON.

NOTE 3.

Excerpts of Buchanite correspondence, written before the proposed Fast of Forty Days.

Elspath Buchan, to Janet Grant, shopkeeper in Irvine.

May 27, 1784.

My dearly beloved in grace here, and in glory hereafter, I write you this to give my love to Mrs Gavin and sister Young. Let both of them know they must give up all things in the world for Christ's kingdom, and that freely, for it is a free-will offering that is accepted by God, and they must not look back if they come here, [New Cample]; so they better settle all their private business before they come away, that they may have nothing to trouble themselves with when here, but wait on the Lord without distraction. Our beloved shepherd, (Rev. Hugh White,) desires me particularly to write to Thomas Neil, not to bring his wife with him here; for he says she shall not be admitted into our society, it being enough to have the devil raging without; were she to be admitted, we would have him within also.—*Mrs Buchan's private Letter-book, in the possession of the author.*

Peter Hunter, to James Gavin, joiner in Irvine.

Nov. 25, 1784

Come off without waiting for any thing, as matters are ripening fast to a conclusion. The Spirit of God on earth, will not stay here on account of worldly business that may hinder you, be what it will; and I am directed by the Spirit of God dwelling with us in the flesh, to assure you, that she will not wish that any of you who has joined in the cause of God, should perish with the world; so do not say the world will not let you come away, and let God work for you. But I tell you that God cannot do any thing for you, for whenever the saints are caught up from the earth, then all will be over. Haste! haste! for your life, I beseech you, and so does all heaven, and all that love the name of God on earth. If any of you do not come, do not let hinder the rest, though it were wife and husband parting with one another Let them come, even if they should creep on their hands and feet, to be here where the Lord dwells in his temple.—*Society's Letter-book.*

From the same to the same.

New Cample, 29th December, 1785

MY DEAR FRIEND,

The disciples who left all and followed Jesus were, no doubt, called fools by the world: this is the same as my companions and myself. I assure you I was as dark as many persons who must have remained in that state had I not seen and heard what I have done from that woman called Mrs Buchan, but who is no other than the woman prophesied of in the 12th chapter of the Revelation of St John. She is the greatest wonder on earth, for she has the mind or spirit of God in her.

You know that all the aspersions and malice of the devil and his angels could devise, both by words and write, have been thrown out and spread abroad against her who is the precious temple wherein God dwells for the last time on earth in its present state. But the mind of God is such a stranger on earth, that when it really appears, it is not known or believed, and this is the present case with my dearest friend in the Lord—the mysterious woman.

Believe me that the only light of God now on earth is at present at this place, and nowhere else.

Elspath Buchan, to James Gavin.

February 19, 1785.

My dear friend in the Son of God, and in the Holy Ghost that the Lord has sent amongst you.—My dear friend, this is a great salvation, notwithstanding the opposition that the devil and the world has made against us. . . . . Thomas Davidson, [their landlord at New Cample,] has shown us a great deal of kindness, even over the belly of all opposition. . . . . But methinks Irvine and Kilmarnock have become the seat of the Beast, and the Parliament Council-house of Hell.—MS. Letter-Book.

NOTE 4.

" It may not be thought out of place here to mention some of the general morbid effects of fasting, more especially as the zeal of one set of well-intentioned enthusiasts, is labouring to restore the fastings of the primitive church as an essential duty. It must be remarked, that these effects naturally vary in different individuals, and in different conditions of the digestive organs; but the following may be regarded as those which result from long fasting. The first are feelings of general debility, which are followed by fever, delirium, violent passion, alternating with the deepest despondency, the temperature of the body is lowered, the respiration becomes fœtid, the secretion of the kidneys is acid and burning, the emaciation of the body is extreme, and, when the fasting has been so protracted as to terminate in death, the stomach has been found contracted. Fasting, it is true, has often been borne for a long time with impunity, in disease, especially in insanity, but in health it cannot be supported many days without risk to life. The strict observance of the Catholic fasts, has often been productive of dyspepsia; and other enthusiasts who have regarded fasting as a virtue, for instance, according to Pinel, the Brahmins, the Fakirs, and Anchorites of the Thebaid, equally suffered from this cause."
—*Thomson's Domestic Management of the Sick-room.* Dr

Elliotson, in his *Human Physiology*, with regard to hunger, in reply to the general opinion that attributes this sensation "to a sympathy of the stomach, with a general feeling of want in the system," remarks, that if hunger arose from fatigue of the stomach, it should be greatest after the laborious act of digestion, and gradually decrease; but, on the contrary, it increases. Were irritation the cause, hunger should be the greatest when the stomach is filled with food. On the whole, therefore, he considers that hunger "may be regarded as a sensation connected with the contracted state of the stomach." On this branch of the subject, he relates the following curious anecdote:—Hippocrates says, that those who abstain from food for seven days, die within that period; and if they do not, and are even prevailed upon to eat and drink, still they perish. Sir William Hamilton, however, saw a girl, sixteen years of age, apparently not in bad health, who was extricated from the ruins of a house at Oppido, in which she had remained eleven days without food; an infant in her arms had died on the fourth day, as the young are never so able to endure abstinence. A moderate supply of water lengthens the life astonishingly. Dr Willan was called to a young man who had voluntarily abstained from every thing but a little water, just flavoured with orange juice, for sixty days; death ensued a fortnight afterwards. Redi cruelly found, that of a number of starved fowls deprived of water none lived beyond the ninth day, whereas one indulged with water, lives upwards of twenty. If the water is not swallowed, but imbibed by the surface or lungs, it may also prolong life. Foderie mentions some workmen who were extricated alive, at the end of fourteen days, from a cold damp cavern in which they had been buried under a ruin. In abstinence, equally great imbecility of mind takes place, as of body; extreme emaciation and œdema of the legs, present a frightful spectacle.

NOTE 5.

Papers connected with the imprisonment of Mrs Buchan and Mr White in the Jail of Dumfries.

Wolviston, County of Durham, 2d Nov. 1840.

DEAR SIR,

The money lodged by my father with the sheriff-clerk in Dumfries, or some person of the name of Short, as appears by the documents which you will find here enclosed, for the liberation of Mrs Buchan and Mr White from the jail of Dumfries, amounted to the sum of one hundred and seven pounds sterling. My father went over to Closeburn about the time it should have been settled, when there was a claim made by Thomas Davidson, farmer, with whom my sisters and I remained during the after part of the fast, for the sum of L.9, which my father paid, that being reasonable. But there was a further charge of between L.60 and L.70 made by Mrs Buchan and Mr White, for the whole family boarding and lodging with them during the time we were at New Cample. This, with some expenses, nearly covered the whole sum of L.107. This sum my father refused to pay, it being quite unreasonable, beyond every thing that could be supposed. Nothing seemed to satisfy them, but the depriving him of every farthing he possessed. On his refusing to pay the demand, the money was arrested in the hands of Mr Short, till the business would be settled in the due course of law.

My father then engaged a Mr William Stewart, factor to Sir —— Monteith of Closeburn Castle, as his agent to act for him, and receive the money as soon as the business could be wound up; and with him he left the bond, and such other documents as he thought necessary. But it lay over till the year 1791, as you will see by the accompanying documents, when White agreed to receive L.15 in payment of the whole sum, to which my father agreed, and frequently wrote to Mr Stewart afterwards respecting the remaining money, but could never get a satisfactory answer from him; and so the business stands at present —&c. &c.

(Signed) THOMAS BRADLEY.

To Joseph Train, Esq,
Loch Vale Cottage, Castle-Douglas.

Papers referred to in the preceding Letter.

Decreet Precept of Poinding.

Jane Grant, alias Muir, and George Hill, (two of the Buchanites,) against Thomas Bradley, 1787. David Armstrong, Esq. of Kirkleton, Advocate, Sheriff-depute of Dumfries-shire, and John Welsh, Esq of Milton, his substitute.

Whereas, upon the first day of February last, Thomas Bradley of Stanton, in the county of Durham, thereafter at New Camphill, in the parish of Closeburn, was deemed and ordained by said sheriff-substitute, sitting in judgment for the time, for the cause therein more fully specified, to make payment to Janet Grant, alias Muir, at New Camphill in the parish of Closeburn, and George Hill there, for themselves and in name and on behalf of the society at New Camphill, commonly called and known by the name of Buchanites, of the sum of fifty-three pounds sixteen shillings, as the balance of a particular account contracted by him with them, libelled upon and proceeded against in due form, and the annual rent of said sum since the 17th day of November last, and in time coming during the non-payment, which sum commences on the 15th July 1789, and ends on the 17th day of November last (1786.) And further, the said Thomas Bradley was decerned by decreet aforesaid, to make payment to the said Janet Grant and George Hill of the sum of ten pounds as the expenses of the said process, together with the fees of extracting said decreet by the clerk of court

Given at Dumfries, this eighth day of March, seventeen hundred and eighty-seven years

Extracted by Ben. Bell, Depute.

By virtue of the preceding decreet, an arrestment was

placed in the hands of Mr Short, writer in Dumfries, on 13th March 1787, by Robert Neilson, sheriff-officer, for the amount therein specified.

Letters from the Rev. Hugh White to Thomas Bradley, Foggy Tower, near Seaton, County of Durham.

(No 1.)

Auchengibbert, Parish of Urr, Kirkcudbrightshire,
30th March 1789.

DEAR THOMAS,

In the latter end of last harvest, I wrote to you concerning a useful recovery of that money in Mr Short's hands. As the letter was so reasonable, and yet no answer from you coming to hand, I am ready to conclude it has never arrived into your hands Consequently, near to the same tenor, notwithstanding the decreet obtained by Janet Grant and George Hill for the detention of £52 in the hands of Mr Short of said money, I, as your trusty friend, have persuaded them both to renounce and give up their claims, provided you are so reasonable and wise for your own interest, as to make me the small allowance of £20, which is £5 less than I thought I ever would have accepted of. Well, do you know, that John Gibson had been long since in possession of £85, and Christian Clement in possession of £20 more of that money, if my activity at law had not defeated them both. In a word, it was owing to my activity that any of that money can be drawn by either you or me; if, then, I have saved the whole, the small sum of £20 to stand against the remaining plea, is a reasonable charge. I know this, that never a friend in Scotland, nor in England neither, has yet set before you a plan, by which you can recover so much of that money, as you can by this plan of agreeing with me. You see, without me the plea cannot be decided, and without decision, the money remains fast in the hands of one who thanks you not for it.

If you agree to this reasonable plan, write to me speedily, and order Mr Stewart to see it executed. The interest of your money in a few years, will amount to all that I am asking—Why not consider these things?—&c. &c.

(Signed)   HUGH WHITE.

From the same to the same.

(No 2)

Auchengibbert, 25th March 1791.

DEAR SIR,

In friendship I would let you know, that the greedy lawyers in Dumfries never mean to part with that money lodged in the hands of Mr Short, if possibly they can keep it. Mr Short, indeed, has had it so long, that he now thinks it is his own; and, let me tell you, that I would rather see it in your hands than in his. Though you stand not in need of it yourself, why might not your children or poor friends have the use of it? and, according to law, there is no way that it can be ended, but by me discharging all claims upon said money, as I told you formerly. Now, in friendship and sincerity, let me tell you again, that, though the plea with M'Cracken be still undecided, and none can tell how much it will cost to end it, yet, if you write expressly to Mr Stewart of Closeburn Castle to give me an order for £15, I shall take my venture of the above-mentioned unfinished plea. If you write immediately the above order to Mr Stewart, I shall discharge all claims, and join with Mr Stewart to compel the greedy lawyers of Dumfries to let go all the impediments upon which they detain the money, so that, in a few weeks you may have it in your own hands, or it may be in the possession of your children. All that I seek against the plea, is not equal to the interest of the money since it has been in the hands of Mr Short.

In friendship the above is written, and if you believe it not, you will afterwards find it to be true.

(Signed)   HUGH WHITE.

P.S.—Had you taken my former advice, the money would have been in your hands long since.

H. W.

The following document, shows that Mr Bradley accepted the offer made in the preceding letter:—

We, the within designed Janet Grant and George Hill, now in Auchengibbert, with consent of the Rev. Hugh White there, in respect it is agreed, that upon payment of £15, to be made to us by William Stewart, Esq., factor on the estate of Closeburn, or by Francis Short, writer in Dumfries, on the part of the within mentioned Thomas Bradley, now in Foggytower, in the county of Durham, which sum, when paid, to be in full of all demands thereon. This we subscribe at Auchengibbert this 19th day of April 1791, before

| Duncan Robertson,
 Joseph Innes, } *Witnesses.* | Janet Grant.
 George Hill.
 Hugh White. |

Dumfries, 20th April 1791.

Received from William Stewart, Esq., a draft upon Francis Short, writer in Dumfries, for the above fifteen pounds, and, as one of the society, being empowered by the persons within named, do hereby grant a discharge to the said Thomas Bradley, and all concerned for ever. I have subscribed these presents before Thomas Cottard and David Newall, writers in Dumfries.

(Signed) Hugh White.

Opinion of Andrew Innes as to the arrestment of Mr Bradley's money, deposited for the liberation of Mrs Buchan and Hugh White from the jail at Dumfries.

Dear Sir,

The information I received by your last visit, was what I long looked for—I mean the recovery of the money lodged with the town-clerk in Dumfries for the liberation of Friend Mother and Mr White from the jail of Dumfries, on account of the claim made against them by John Gibson and James Stewart, amounting to £85. I have since been surprised at receiving Mr White's two letters from you by post—they are both in his own handwriting. They let you see his treacherous dealings with Mr Bradley; they are no more than I expected. By using fair promises and falsehood, he expected to make Thomas believe he was his friend, because he wanted the power to do otherwise; he pretended to use all his skill to restore to Thomas the money deposited by him for the benefit of his family, when the reverse was the case; he boasts of preventing Janet Grant and George Hill getting that £52, that I believe never had any existence. Christian Clements' were settled long before Thomas Bradley left England; but I have no doubt of his using his skill to prevent John Gibson getting the £85 claimed by him and John Stewart, but they were all out of the way then, and had nothing to do with the money deposited by Thomas Bradley to liberate him from prison, to meddle with which was both ungrateful, unjust, and unchristian. The more information I receive respecting this affair, it has the worse appearance in my eyes.

(Signed)   Andrew Innes.

NOTE 6.

Parallel between Luckie Buchan and Mother Lee.

The blasphemous pretensions, heresies, and circumstances in the life of Mrs Buchan, bear a more striking resemblance to those of Ann Lee, than to the fantasies of Joanna Southcote,[1] the theological system of Madame Bourignon, or the tenets of any other female impostor with whose history I am acquainted.[2]

Ann Lee was born at Manchester, in the year 1735. She was the daughter of a blacksmith, and was quite illiterate.[3]

Elspath Simpson was born near Banff, in the year 1738.

[1] Buck's Theological Dictionary.
[2] Edinburgh Christian Instructor, for March 1833.
[3] Appendix to the Trial of the Rev. Edward Irving before the presbytery of Annan, p. 102

She was the daughter of an alehouse-keeper, and received almost no education.[1]

In the year 1774, Ann Lee was enlightened by a special revelation of signs, visions, and extraordinary manifestations.[2]

In the year 1774, also, Elspath Simpson was enabled, as it was affirmed, by the power of God, to live for some weeks without food, when all things became new to her except the mortal flesh and blood[3]

In the year 1780, Mother Lee, as she was now called, went with a few devotees to America, and became the founder of a sect of fanatics at New Lebanon, still known by the name of "Shakers."[4]

In the year 1783, Luckie Buchan, as she was then called, arrived at Irvine, in Ayrshire, and became the founder of a knot of visionaries, since called Buchanites.

Mother Lee gave herself out as an incarnation of Christ in the female form. Hence the image and likeness of the Eternal Mother was formed in her, as the first-born daughter, as truly as the image and likeness of the Eternal Father was formed in the Lord Jesus, the first-born son.[5]

Luckie Buchan gave herself out to be the Spirit of God, or third person in the Godhead. Christ, she called her elder brother, as being the second person in the Godhead. One

---

[1] Mrs Buchan's Letter to the Rev. Francis Okley of Northampton. —Buchanite Letter-book, p. 87.

[2] Evans' Sketch of the Denominations of the Christian World. London edition, 1808, p 209.

[3] Letter to the Rev Francis Okley of Northampton —Letter-book, p 88.

[4] At the date of the American publication from which the particulars respecting Ann Lee are taken, the sect called Shakers, founded by her, could boast of sixteen stations in various parts of the United States of America, amounting to 4000 souls —Appendix to the Trial of Edward Irving. According to a more recent work, this sect have six regular societies in New England, six in the state of New York, and five in Ohio, Kentucky, and Indiana, amounting to 5000 souls.—Stewart s America.

[5] Trial of Edward Irving, p. 106; Buck's Theological Dictionary, see "Shakers."

APPENDIX. 255

of her daughters, she said, was an incarnation of Christ, the other of the Holy Ghost.[1]

Mother Lee gave herself out to be the mother of all the elect, and the woman mentioned in the 12th chapter of the Revelation of St John.[2]

Luckie Buchan declared herself to be the mysterious woman mentioned in the 12th chapter of the Revelation, in whom the light of God was restored to the earth.[3]

Mother Lee declared that the second coming of Christ and day of redemption was nigh, even at the very door; and the meetings of her followers resounded with cries to God for his kingdom to come.[4]

Luckie Buchan was to meet the Lord in the clouds, at his second coming, with her followers, and to take them thence to heaven without tasting death[5]

The countenance of Mother Lee shone with glory when under the inspiration of the Holy Ghost.[6]

Mother Buchan was the light of God, and her countenance shone so bright, at the great agitation, as to dazzle the eyes of all beholders.[7]

Mother Lee professed the power of communicating the Holy Spirit by laying on of hands.[8]

Mother Buchan professed the power of communicating the

---

[1] Divine Dictionary, pp 3, 4 " It appears, by autograph letters of this woman, (i e. Mrs Buchan,) and from the correspondence of some of her followers, which we have seen, that by herself and by them she was considered as being the Spirit of God dwelling in the flesh; as being, in short, the incarnation of the Holy Spirit "—Statistical Account of Scotland: Irvine, Ayrshire, edition 1842

[2] Trial of Edward Irving, p. 103; Evans' Sketch of the Denominations of the Christian World, p 209; Buck's Theological Dictionary, vide " Shakers "

[3] Divine Dictionary [4] Ibid.

[5] Trial of Edward Irving.

[6] Divine Dictionary. Her proper cognomen was Friend Mother in the Lord

[7] Divine Dictionary, p. 31

[8] Trial of Edward Irving, p. 104.

Holy Spirit by breathing on the person selected for that purpose.[1]

Mother Lee's followers vented their enthusiasm in jumping and turning round for an hour or two at a time; this violent exertion of the body bringing on shaking, from which they derived their name.[2]

Mother Buchan's followers vented their enthusiasm by singing rhymes of their own composition.[3]

When Mother Lee breathed her last, elder John Hockwell saw her mount a golden chariot, drawn by four milk-white steeds, which flew away with the speed of lightning.[4]

And when Mother Buchan had been dead six days, Mr White saw her carried away by an angel.

NOTE 7.

(Copy)

Extract of Deed of Settlement by Andrew Innes and Spouse, in favour of Duncan Robertson and others, and

Dated $\frac{3}{14}$ *January* 1819.   *Stamp*, 10s. 4d.
Regt. 1 ...... 1828.   *Copies*, 12s. 11d.

At Kirkcudbright, the first day of January 1828, Sir Alexander Gordon, Knight, sheriff-depute, and William Ire-

---

[1] Divine Dictionary, page 30. "She professed to have the power of conferring the Holy Spirit; and those to whom this was imparted, were not only held to be securely fixed in a state of grace, beyond the possibility of declension or of falling away, but they were even deemed incapable of committing any iniquity. The overt act, implying criminality in others, could not be committed by them; for it was one of their dogmas, that the seat of corruption, after regeneration, is what in Scripture is termed "flesh," which is explained as distinct both from "body" and "soul"—Christian Journal, vol. v. p. 308.

[2] See the Duc de Rouchfoucault's Travels through America, vol i, and New York Theological Magazine, for November and December 1795.

[3] Divine Dictionary, pp. 114-117.

[4] Trial of Edward Irving, p. 106.

land of Burley, sheriff-substitute of the stewartry of Kirkcudbright, officiating sheriff-substitute, compeared David Morrison, writer in Kirkcudbright, as procurator for the granters of the said deed of settlement, and craved that the same might be registered in the stewart books according to law, the words being as follows :—

We, Andrew Innes, and Katherine Gardner, his spouse, residing at Newhouse of Crocketford, in the stewartry of Kirkcudbright, with the advice and consent of each other, for the favour and esteem we have for the following persons, have resolved to settle and dispose of our estate to them as underwritten. Therefore, we do by these presents give and grant to Margaret Innes, Duncan Robertson, Christian Robertson and Janet Robertson, his sisters, and Jane Watt, residing in Crocketford aforesaid, and to Ann Buchan, alias Goldie, residing in Maxwellton, in the parish of Troqueer, for their joint liferent use and advantage in the event of their surviving us, and to the survivor or longest liver, and to his or her heirs for ever, all and whole of our land at Crocketford, in the parish of Kirkpatrick-Durham, disposed to me, the said Andrew Innes, by the said William Ireland, Esq., sheriff-substitute, conform to disposition dated the fourth day of July 1812, which land is situated between the toll-road leading through Crocketford to New Galloway and the march of Meiklelarg, being bounded by the toll-road on the south and north, and to George Kidd, and the other feuars before named, conform to minutes or missives thereanent, which land here disposed of extends to one acre, one rood, and sixteen falls or thereby, in liferent only, together with the whole parts and pendicles pertaining thereto.* As also

* Immediately following the above words there are the following words on the margin of the original deed, in the handwriting of Andrew Innes. "It never was intended (by Andrew Innes) that the park whereof he has the rights in his own name, was to be included in this deed of settlement beyond the lifetime of the last survivor, so that all privileges granted to the heirs of the last survivor respecting it are void and of none effect Subscribed (and signed) by Andrew Innes, Jan. 19, 1825."

R

all and sundry other lands and goods, of whatever denomination, which belongs to us, or may belong to us at the time of our deaths respectively, together with all contracts, bonds, bills, &c.; but declaring always, that by acceptation thereof, the persons aforesaid, or the survivors of them, shall be bound out of the first and readiest of the estate and effects hereby conveyed, to pay all our just and lawful debts, sick-bed and funeral charges. The aforesaid persons shall be entitled to enter upon said liferent upon the death of me the said Andrew Innes, and shall enjoy the same with me, the said Katherine Gardner; and, in consideration of these presents, and from similar motives, we the aforesaid persons, have unanimously agreed to leave to the said Andrew Innes a proportional interest in means, goods, and estate of which we may be possessed at the time of our respective deaths, and do severally give, grant, and assign in favour of the said Andrew Innes and Katherine Gardner, all and sundry goods, gear, debts, and sums of money of which we may be possessed at the time of our deaths respectively, but reserving full power and liberty for each of us to alter and revoke these presents, in whole or in part, with the concurrence and knowledge of each other or a majority of us, at any time we may think proper; and we, the said Andrew Innes and Katherine Gardner, reserve to ourselves, or the survivor of us, the use of these premises and effects during our lifetime respectively. And further, to the end that the said interests may be secured to the said persons respectively, and the said Andrew Innes, hereby require you my baillies to go to the said lands, and there give and deliver real and corporeal possession of all and whole the lands aforesaid, lying as before described, to the persons aforesaid.

In witness whereof these presents, wrote upon this and three preceding pages on stamped paper, by Benjamin Blake, clerk to John Sanders, writer in Dumfries, and subscribed by Andrew Innes, Katherine Gardner, Duncan Robertson, Margaret Innes, Jean Watt, and George Kidd, at Crocketford, the third day of January 1820 years, in presence of Robert Smith and John Smith, both shopkeepers at Crocketford, and the said John Sanders, and by the said Ann Buchan or Goldie, at Dumfries, the fourth day of January in the year aforesaid, before these witnesses, the said John Sanders and Benjamin Blake.

Extracted by David Melville.

(*Note at the foot of this deed in the handwriting of Andrew Innes.*)

After having deliberately considered this deed of settlement, and taken the advice of several men experienced in the law, who have all advised me to disannul this deed altogether in and during my own lifetime, because its preservation could only be the means of dispute and contention; and as the retention of the land was the unanimous wish of all concerned, except Ann Buchan, who never contributed one penny to procure any part of the property, but hath already received, in money and otherwise, more than the share of any other person would have amounted to had the property been equally divided at the time, a statement of which I have made out on another paper, to satisfy any impartial judge that I am well entitled to put an end to the above deed, and I hereby declare it null and void, and of none effect in all its parts. I have written the above with my own hand, for the satisfaction of all whom it may concern, upon this tenth day of August, in the year eighteen hundred and thirty-two years, and subscribed before these witnesses.

Margaret Innes, a party.
Cathrin Gardner's mark, +
 a party in the deed also.

George Murray, *Witness*.
Wm. Charters, *Witness*.

THE END.

EDINBURGH: BALLANTYNE AND HUGHES.

Lightning Source UK Ltd.
Milton Keynes UK
UKOW06f0640020114

223840UK00010B/355/P